GETTING E-COMMERCE RIGHT

How to plan, build and grow online sales

Stephen Fry
Michael Bird
Award-Winning Digital Experts

SPIN VENTURES, INC.

GETTING E-COMMERCE RIGHT | How to Plan, Build and Grow Online Sales

© 2019 Spin Ventures, Inc.

ISBN 978-1-687-319418

For information and distribution rights, royalties, derivative works or licensing opportunities on behalf of this content or work, please contact Spin Ventures, Inc. at the address shown below or via email at info@GettingE-CommerceRight.com.

COMPANIES, ORGANIZATIONS, INSTITUTIONS AND INDUSTRY PUBLICATIONS: Quantity discounts are available on bulk purchases of this book for reselling, educational purposes, subscription incentives, gifts, sponsorship or fundraising. Special books or book excerpts can also be created to fit specific needs such as private labeling with your logo on the cover and a message from the author printed inside. Contact Spin Ventures, Inc. at 877-225-4200 for more information.

Authors are available by email: Stephen Fry, sfry@spindustry.com and Michael Bird, mbird@spindustry.com.

Spin Ventures, Inc.
1370 NW 114th Street, Suite 300
Des Moines, IA 50325

This book was printed in the United States of America

Formatting: Jarrod L. Edge, Pamela J. Smith

Dedication

This book is dedicated to the leaders of large organizations who are tired of using old fashioned sales models and are ready to take a giant leap forward with modern E-Commerce. The rewards are worthy of the effort.

Acknowledgments

We take this opportunity to thank our wives, families, amazing team members at Spindustry, friends, business partners and most of all our amazing clients for making this book possible. Without their trust and support over the past nearly 25 years, we couldn't possibly have the experience to share the ideas in this book.

Steve and Michael

Table of Contents

What is E-Commerce?

The phrase *E-Commerce* is generally well understood today, though its complexity is reaching farther and deeper across business and consumer transactions. If you're not leveraging E-Commerce to sell your products and services to your ideal customers, you're missing out on opportunities to increase revenues, profitability and geographic reach.

> *E-Commerce encompasses the use of the Internet to attract, connect and sell products and services to resellers and end-users.*

Why should you care about E-Commerce? Because E-Commerce is reshaping how businesses interact with customers, prospects and partners. If you're not yet at least experimenting with E-Commerce in your organization, you are literally putting the future of your company at risk.

This book will help you start the process of bringing E-Commerce into your business for the first time or successfully expand upon what you're already doing.

If you don't have time to read this book, give it to a designated leader in your organization who does and then listen to them when they come back to you with ideas.

Introduction

For nearly twenty-five years, we've had the opportunity to work alongside many companies. We've served some of the largest companies on the planet, some of the smallest and quite a few in between. At times our journey has been challenging—like in the early days having to educate our prospects and clients that the internet is for real. For the most part, our work has been incredibly rewarding.

So why are we writing this book? Simple. We love helping companies grow and it's frustrating to see great organizations missing out on opportunities to increase sales. If you own or run a company and you follow the guidance we offer in the pages of this book, you will see positive results. There are so many possibilities for business owners and leaders to leverage the power of E-Commerce to increase sales, improve margins and genuinely connect better with sales channel partners and end-consumers alike.

Candidly, we focus our work these days with companies that can invest enough to do E-Commerce the right way. Typical annual budgets for our clients range from $150,000 to $1,000,000 plus. But any business seeking to use E-Commerce to sell products and services can find value in the challenges we offer in this book.

It is understandable that for many organizations, the idea of doing all the things we describe in this book is just too overwhelming. If that sounds like you, we simply counsel you to take small steps. You can still find a worthwhile return by taking on one (or a few) of the challenges that follow. If you need help, find an experienced partner to lead your organization through the process.

We've designed this book to be easy for you to get through. We outline many common challenges that you will face. To make the information simple to digest, you'll see that we group these challenges into three distinct areas of focus.

PLANNING Your E-Commerce. In this section, we'll map out the steps you need to take to plan for a successful E-Commerce development cycle and launch. You'll discover some of the most common E-Commerce challenges typical organizations face. We also address how E-Commerce can bring an enhanced level of support, efficiency and cost savings to your business.

BUILDING Your E-Commerce. Once you've put the plan in place to add or elevate E-Commerce in your business, it's time to get building. You'll learn how to establish a team that can effectively oversee the development process. We share the key functionalities required to maximize digital commerce success. You'll find a series of challenges you may be facing and specific direction you can use to find new sales growth opportunities and higher margins.

GROWING Your E-Commerce. Now that E-Commerce is an integral part of your business, it's time to focus on increasing online sales. Adding new customers is surely a worthy endeavor, but so is increasing the average value of each customer's order. In this section, we offer several ideas that can be deployed to expedite new sales growth.

If you find specific challenges in this book of interest, feel free to skip to those that are most relevant to you. We want to genuinely help your business. This book is different than other business books that simply impart theory. We want you to use this book and companion website as an ongoing reference guide. www.GettingE-CommerceRight.com. The site will provide additional information about making your business stronger using innovative E-Commerce strategies.

To make this book easier for you and your team to use, we're including a **1-in-30 Days Action Step** for each challenge. Each action step gives you one thing you can accomplish in the next thirty days to move forward with a particular challenge. Use the 1-in-30 Action Steps to help you explore what you're doing today and why. Then start to look at how you can implement positive changes going forward that will help your company meet and exceed future growth goals.

As a manufacturer, distributor, wholesaler or retailer, you face both opportunities and competition. If you're willing to make an investment in E-Commerce, we know you can generate more sales and grow your business. You'll also end up with happier customers because they can find what they want and engage with your company on their own time.

So, grab a notepad and let's get started. There's more high-margin business out there if you're willing to follow the steps outlined in this book.

Good luck and let us know how you're able to grow your business leveraging E-Commerce!

The Digital Ecosystem

Before we dive into the business challenges and opportunities E-Commerce provides, we want to share more about the digital ecosystem with you. This section will serve as an active glossary of terms that we use throughout the book. First, we define different parts of the digital ecosystem and then we discuss the process of creating digital assets that should surround E-Commerce, like customer portals, dealer portals, landing pages, digital marketing, videos and more. Our hope is that this information will help orient you to what the digital ecosystem has to offer as you work with your internal team or with external experts.

A Little History

For many of you, your first experience with "digital" was likely an America Online (AOL) email account. Back then, email was little more than a complement to your phone, fax and in-person communication. Soon thereafter, email became a vital tool for doing business. The ability to communicate with friends, family and business associates expanded greatly. Then, company brochure websites emerged as the next step in being a part of the digital world. Back then websites were viewed as the behind-the-scenes or unofficial newswire of a company, usually maintained exclusively by IT departments. Over time, however, websites have evolved into the virtual front door of business.

As companies began getting comfortable with their websites—which took some time and often a lot of compromise between IT and marketing—we saw social channels spring to life. Several different platforms were introduced, each of which urged companies to engage in this new communication style. More recently, social channels have given companies the ability to provide more information and initiate an online conversation with their constituents for the first time. Not unlike websites, it has taken organizations a long time to fully embrace social media for the value it offers. Quite a number of companies, still today, are not taking advantage of social media, while still others are doing nothing but the absolute basics.

With powerful smartphones in virtually every pocket, email, the web and social media are an integral part of our daily routines. Gone are the days of dial-up—though we recall, fondly, the cool telephone tones we heard as we logged onto the Internet. Now, with the tap of a finger, we can communicate with almost any person or company on the planet 24/7. The expectation that a business listens and responds to its customers and sales channel partners has never been higher.

Today's Digital Business Ecosystem

E-Commerce experiences, websites, dealer portals, email, YouTube and social media are just the tip of the iceberg of the digital ecosystem. There are many other important components that make up the ever-growing digital world. Here are some of the more important examples:

Microsites and Landing Pages. While a microsite is a small website with a few pages and a landing page is typically just a single page, each serves the same general purpose. These small websites provide niche content on the Internet that is intended to attract potential, highly-targeted visitors. When used effectively, these sites focus on a single idea and encourage visitors to take a directed, clear next step, like filling out a form, downloading a white paper or calling into a customer service/sales telephone number.

You've probably heard the term *content marketing*. This is the use of niche-focused information placed on a microsite, landing page or website that is designed to attract, educate and engage visitors (buyers), who need the specific kind of product or service you offer. Microsites and landing pages are typically constructed at modest expense and the results they derive can be measured with great accuracy.

Intuitive Search. Too many companies are ignoring the importance of a quality search. Studies vary but it's not unusual to find that a website's search is the method that 50 percent or more visitors use to find what they want. Creating intuitive navigation is still vitally important, but so is creating a search functionality that returns the right results.

Blogs. A blog is a website used to post articles and opinions that are relevant to readers. Blogs are generally designed for one-way interaction with desired audiences. Unlike a discussion board that facilitates a crossflow of information between different parties, blogs are typically authored by organizational leaders and employees. For the purpose of sharing company information, the content of blogs should be written with a voice and tone that matches the personality of your organization. While the content shared can certainly be business-related, often the most effective blogs are those that showcase the personality and culture of a business. Sharing interesting stories about your company and team or talking about the philanthropic efforts you support are examples of how you can more deeply engage with visitors. Readers can provide commentary, but with blogs, there is typically minimal back and forth interaction. Recognize that your blog content can often reveal a different and more humanizing perspective about your organization than your primary website.

Search Engines/Organic Search Engine Optimization. Search engines make it easy for people to find exactly what they're looking for online. The goal of search engine optimization is to make your content easy for the major search engines to find and index. You want your company to show up as one of the first organic results when prospects search in Google for the products and services you offer. Organic results don't cost anything, though you must continually do the right things to get and keep your company's good rankings. This goal is achieved in several ways, but it starts by having your website created using a search-friendly infrastructure. As content is added, you'll want to make sure that it includes the high-ranking keywords that match the phrases your prospective customers are typing into the search engines. There is certainly more to this, but you get the basic idea.

Pay-per-click (PPC)/Google Ads. In addition to ranking well in the search engines organically, you can *buy* your way to visibility. The easiest way to get to the top of the search engine results is to pay for clicks using Google Ads. Other search engines function in a similar manner. Yes, you'll have to pay when (but only when) an online visitor clicks on your company's listing, but if you want your company's products and services to be listed at the top of the results, you can. Best of all, unlike traditional advertising, you only pay for the visitors that click your ad, not everyone that sees your ad.

We hear some business leaders say that they think paid ads aren't as valuable as organic listings. The reality is that statistics prove that thinking to be wrong. People do click on paid ads, especially when the messaging of the ad is written in a highly relevant way that matches their needs. Savvy web users often look at sponsored ads first, knowing that each company displayed is paying to be there. If you need more proof, just look at how Google's stock has performed.

Well-designed display ads that are shown on targeted websites can be a great way to reach prospective customers, dealers and employees who have an interest in the content offered. Creating paid content in an "advertorial" format attracts online visitors who are looking for specific information about a product, service or problem. Trade associations, industry sites and social media channels all offer good websites to place banner ads.

Competitor Conquesting. This is a phenomenon that involves bidding on a competitor business' name (or brand, model, product, etc.). There are some considerations to be made, but this can be a very effective and economical way to get your business/products in front of your competitor's prospects. Just make sure you give such ads a clear message that draws visitors to your business.

Videos. YouTube allows companies to create their own YouTube Channel to showcase videos to a public or private audience. Public videos can be educational (how-to, product demonstration or manufacturing process) or they may highlight your company's people, philanthropy, philosophy, etc.) From an engagement perspective, good videos are a great way to connect to your audiences. It's worth noting that YouTube is one of the largest search engines as well.

Stages of Web Development

A quick online search will provide a myriad of books written on various web development processes. Because that's not what this book is about, here is your crash course.

1. A good web development process will always begin with *strategy* and *goals*. A new website should not be built simply because you are bored with your current one. Before embarking on a new site, review and understand what is and what is not working with your current site by reviewing your Google Analytics and other feedback from visitors and your own team. To get the best results, it's important to have documented, *quantifiable* business goals that detail what you want to achieve with the new site. Then, on at least a quarterly basis, check the progress of your site against the stated goals. Like all goals, making your web/E-Commerce expectations clear at the beginning, followed by ongoing check-ins, will dramatically increase your chances for success.

2. As a part of the strategic analysis process, you and your development team should be identifying groups of customers and partners who will use your website/E-Commerce store. Focus on *why* these different types of visitors will use the site. These groups can be named different things, but the most common term we hear is *personas*. Regardless of what you choose to call them, make sure you know their specific business needs. A common challenge we see in our work with clients is that when thinking about E-Commerce, organizations view their content from the "inside-out" rather than from the "outside-in." To solve this, when writing any content for your website/store, put yourself in the shoes of your visitors, who may not know your business or your internal jargon. Then imagine the questions they have or information they need to accurately learn about

your business, your products, your processes and what it takes to build a good relationship with your business.

3. After clarifying your quantifiable goals and the information needed to measure and support them, creating a site map is usually the next step. The site map will provide a high level "org chart" view of the eventual E-Commerce site and identify where different types of content will be housed.

4. With the site map completed, the next step is creating wireframes or storyboards for individual pages of your new site. Wireframes add page-level detail to the site map. The wireframing process will help your team visualize what elements are needed on each page. Having to make choices about what information goes where forces you and your team to think through your business processes and determine what different audiences want to see. Wireframing is typically an iterative process, meaning there is back and forth between the E-Commerce development team and project sponsor, as features and functions are evaluated and finalized. Plan on this work taking a few weeks—or longer—for more complex E-Commerce sites—if you are doing it right. Using wireframes to determine functionality saves money in the long run because they minimize expensive programming rework.

5. Once you have approved the wireframes for your new E-Commerce site, the development team will create a mock-up of primary site pages. Most often the team will create the home page and one or more inside pages to visually demonstrate the look and feel of the

new site. Additional mock-ups, sometimes called design comps may be needed, depending upon the complexity of your new site. After any desired revisions, full E-Commerce site design can begin.

6. With clearly defined goals, a site map, wireframes and a final design direction confirmed and approved, the creation of a website often then splits into multiple, concurrent paths.

> *Technical Design.* The design team will need to take the approved mock-ups and wireframes and create HTML and other required technical files (CSS, JavaScript, etc.) that result in an E-Commerce website that can function on the Internet.

> *Programming/Development.* The programming team, sometimes called "the developers," takes the HTML and associated files and connects them to databases or other sources of content. These technicians also develop interactivity, like site search, product cross-reference tables, configurators, order-by-schematics, forms, merchandising, promotions, calls-to-action, cart functionality, reporting tools and content management systems.

> *Integration.* One of the most challenging parts of any E-Commerce effort is integrating your online store with backend systems. This includes ERP platforms, accounting systems, freight calculation software, sales tax software, inventory software and similar services. If you don't have an

experienced development team that knows how to do this properly, you're asking for big headaches.

Product Content Team. With the final E-Commerce site map and wireframes in hand, your product content team—expert(s) in your company's products—will be needed to determine the right product taxonomy (categories/sub-categories) attributes for each product. Additionally, this team will need to gather and prepare product descriptions, product imagery, product kits, product cross-references and more. They will need to begin the process of gathering, curating or creating needed content early in the timeline. Typically, about midway through the development process, your new E-Commerce site will be ready to receive initial product content. During this trial and error period, everyone can start to see how the new site looks with your company's actual product content. Depending on budget, it may be more appropriate to have the development company's technical design team load at least the initial site content, as they can make sure each page looks good and works well with your new E-Commerce site's overall design.

Search Engine Optimization ("SEO"). A separate team can be working simultaneously on *keyword research* and *content optimization*, which will help search engines find and index your products on your live E-Commerce website. If you're going from an old site to a new site, you'll want to pay careful attention to minimize the loss of any search engine visibility you've already gained. Your team or development partner can create what are called "redirects" to refer new site pages to existing search engine results. This SEO team will also work with the design and development teams to make sure that the structure of the new website accommodates their needs to maximize search engine visibility. It's important to recognize that the major search engines are constantly updating their algorithms, so you will need to have the flexibility to adapt to these dynamic changes and maximize your SEO effectiveness.

Technical Support. Support technicians will be needed to handle the final backend site needs and to configure the selected hosting services upon which your site will reside. Discussions surrounding the hosting of your site should be a part of upfront planning. As development begins, hosting plans must be revisited to see if any of the initial assumptions have changed. There will be a checklist of other details to consider. For E-Commerce stores, several in-depth conversations with the right parties will be required to finalize the desired methods of moving data to and from the new online store to your organization's backend systems.

7. As the new E-Commerce site nears completion, quality assurance and testing will intensify. We strongly recommend that testing be done throughout the design and development process to identify any underlying issues long before they can become big problems. As the site/store starts to really take shape, it will be useful to

move it from the development platform to a staging platform. There, the site will not be in flux as developers work on it. Note that even though you and your team can access the new E-Commerce site, it will not be available to the public just yet. Immediately prior to the site's launch, final testing should be done in what's called the production environment.

8. It is important to perform full retesting immediately after launch and then regularly for the first 30 to 90 days following launch. After that point, a quarterly or semi-annual level of deep testing should suffice, unless you're experiencing problems. This testing regimen will minimize the likelihood of product content abnormalities or unseen errors.

While not an exhaustive history of digital, glossary of all things Internet or a manual on E-Commerce development, we hope this overview helps you understand the complexities of the digital ecosystem. This information will align with our recommendations and allow you to make good decisions about leveraging internal digital team members or engaging an external development partner in the future.

Section 1
PLANNING Your E-Commerce

Section 1 – PLANNING Your E-Commerce

If you're like most business owners and leaders, your top priorities come down to three basic things. The first is understanding your customers so that you can offer products and services they want to buy. The second is giving your employees the tools they need to do their jobs well and efficiently. The third is seeking opportunities to grow your business with innovative ideas. To be successful in business today, it's imperative to always be looking at new ways to serve your current customers and attract new buyers.

In this section, we take a closer look at some of the challenges typical organizations face when planning new E-Commerce experiences or enhancing existing online sales. The challenges in *Planning Your E-Commerce* include:

- Involving the right people in your E-Commerce planning?
- Establishing specific goals for E-Commerce
- The necessity of upfront analysis
- Hiring an internal team or an external partner?
- Adding direct-to-consumer business to a B2B model
- Selling online to your usual customers is still E-Commerce
- Buying or building your new E-Commerce platform?
- Determining what your customers really want
- Enhancing sales channel support
- Handling customer service in a better way
- Keeping up with digital regulations
- Looking at your current marketing
- Finding innovative ways to pay for E-Commerce
- When is the best time to launch E-Commerce?

Section 1 – PLANNING Your E-Commerce

CHALLENGE:
Involving the right people in your E-Commerce planning
Putting the right members of your team on a committee to oversee your E-Commerce planning, development and ongoing growth is key to long-term success.

If your business has never had E-Commerce, it is important to assemble a team of knowledgable people from across multiple departments. This steering committee should be made up of team members who are encouraged to freely express their ideas, experience and potential concerns.

The very first person needed is an executive sponsor. Depending on the size of the organization, this individual might be the owner, president or a division leader. Regardless of who it is, this individual must have ultimate control over how E-Commerce will function within the company and be able to secure an adequate budget to plan, develop and grow your online sales efforts.

One word of caution about the executive sponsor role. This person should remain engaged in how your business conducts E-Commerce from this point forward. This doesn't mean that they have to attend every meeting, but they do need to have a complete understanding of how your digital commerce will impact each part of your business. As key decisions about your new E-Commerce site are made, the executive sponsor needs to back up the team.

On occasion we see executive sponsors attend initial planning sessions for new E-Commerce projects and then disappear until near the launch of a new store. Very late in the process, they start questioning why decisions have been made. This is incredibly tough on the team and development partner if you have one. Creating new E-Commerce for a business involves countless choices. When done properly, a lot of thought, research and best practices go into a new site. While a sponsor's personal preferences may be interesting, they should not drive E-Commerce decision-making. Our guidance is to have the executive sponsor stay involved to avoid confusion and team frustration after they've done all the hard work to get to launch.

Once you have identified the executive sponsor, you'll want to invite a representative from finance, production, IT, sales, marketing and customer service departments. An ideal team size is 6-10 people. From our experience, if you get more than 10 people, your meetings will be cumbersome.

The people selected should really understand how their department works. They should know where information can be obtained, including:

- Customer lists and account numbers
- Product descriptions and specifications
- Product images, videos and manuals
- Schematic drawings of equipment
- Pricing tiers by customer/dealer type
- Promotional offers (and any restrictions)
- Inventory information
- Special order rules and processes
- Product packaging, including dimensions and weights
- Handling hazardous materials orders
- How to handle partial order shipments
- Shipping methods, rules and guidelines
- Collecting applicable federal, state and local taxes
- Applicable payment terms
- Payment processing
- Customer service of orders
- Returns processing
- Warranty registration
- Data security
- Website/E-Commerce hosting

Some of the expertise required to handle these many topics may be found in external partners. The point is that you need to assemble a team of experts who can navigate the entire sales process and determine what portion, if not all of it, can be handled online.

For most companies, the information needed to launch a new E-Commerce site is significant and almost always more time consuming to gather than anticipated. If your company engages in proper planning, clearly defining what is needed and who is responsible, this will make this process much less daunting.

The E-Commerce steering committee may need to continue meeting well beyond the launch of the E-Commerce site to oversee future modifications and enhancements. Because of inherent departmental knowledge and the experience gained from planning to launch, each team member should be able to offer effective guidance on how to keep online sales running smoothly and respond to unplanned situations that may arise once E-Commerce is underway.

Determine who the executive sponsor is for your prospective E-Commerce initiative. If it's you, great. Be a good leader by staying involved throughout the process. Regardless of who the executive sponsor is, once that individual is identified, sit down and have a conversation about the specific people in your company who would be positive contributors to an E-Commerce steering committee. You want to find people who have a lot of knowledge about how things work in their department and internal experts who aren't afraid to respectfully share their thoughts.

Having a list in hand of the people you want to serve on such a committee will get some initial energy flowing towards your new E-Commerce efforts. Once the steering committee is assembled, move quickly to have an initial meeting where high-level goals and expectations can be outlined.

Section 1 – PLANNING Your E-Commerce

CHALLENGE:
Establishing specific goals for E-Commerce success
When you clearly define what success looks like for your E-Commerce investment, you create a target that everyone should be able to understand and embrace.

If you've decided that it's time to start selling or enhance the sale of your products or services online, hopefully, you have a good idea of what you want to get from the effort. For many, it's an increase in profitable sales. For others, it's the desire to serve customers in a new and better way.

Regardless of what is driving your E-Commerce push, sit down and detail expectations in a quantifiable way. If you've been assigned the responsibility of building and deploying online sales in your business, work with the executive sponsor or business owner to document exactly how your E-Commerce initiatives will be evaluated.

If the business owner or executive sponsor cannot define what digital commerce success looks like, take a break from the process to get these details determined.

When we talk about establishing specific goals, we do mean *specific*. It's not enough to say, "I want more sales." You need to define precisely what you want. For example, you might say, "To make the investment in our E-Commerce worthwhile, we need to see an increase in product sales of 10 percent within the first 12 months." To the degree that you can break down your goals into smaller data sets that can be easily tracked and verified, the happier you (or the business owner) will be as you report goal progress updates.

Goals can cover a lot of different areas of an E-Commerce effort.

Far beyond dollars, you may be interested in goals that track:

- Happier customers (discovered from surveys and conversations)
- Fewer returns
- Better relationships with suppliers
- Reduction in customer service calls
- The addition of new product lines
- Augmenting offline sales gaps with online sales
- Moving stale inventory
- Keeping employees busy (reducing layoffs)

You get the idea. E-Commerce has the ability to help an organization in ways that go far beyond just more sales and profits—though we get that this is the primary reason for getting into online sales. Making sure that the goals for E-Commerce are well documented and shared is the proper way to ensure that your efforts will be successful.

Your marketing team—or external marketing partner—need to know your goals as well so they can tailor their efforts to achieve the expectations. We've seen too many companies running E-Commerce without goals or with expectations that can be easily misinterpreted. As the importance of E-Commerce sales moves from experimentation to vital, we are fortunately seeing a change towards more well-defined goals.

It's reasonable for goals and expectations to be updated over time. Make certain they are measurable and that everyone on the team—and company—have a clear understanding of what is expected. When goals are achieved, be sure an celebrate those victories. If results fall short of a goal, explore the probable cause. Based on the findings, you may need to make an adjustment in your E-Commerce process or recalibrate future goal expectations.

Over the years we've learned that the best way to get to a set of realistic, quantifiable goals is to investigate what success looks like to the executive sponsor or owner of the business. Ask the business owner the following:

> *"Imagine it's a year after the launch of your new (or latest) E-Commerce site and we're celebrating its success. Tell me, specifically, what has happened in the last year."*

Using this approach, you'll often get feedback that can be converted into specific goals. You may also learn other drivers behind the desire to push E-Commerce that aren't goal-related but can be used to inform decision-making around the E-Commerce efforts your company is making.

Section 1 – PLANNING Your E-Commerce

CHALLENGE:
The necessity of upfront analysis
One sure way to get your E-Commerce off to a good start is with proper analysis before any decisions are made or development begins.

Like any new endeavor, it's best to do some analysis of options before you get into the work. Starting anew or elevating your E-Commerce is no different. In fact, if you don't do some serious analysis on the front end, we can guarantee you that you'll end up spending more money than you should.

Fortunately, most business owners and leaders understand this point. Probably because this same requirement applies to other areas of the business as well.

Analysis should be comprehensive and be performed by people that have experience doing E-Commerce well—and, importantly, in the recent past. Once you've identified the right people to help guide the analysis, you can expect them to dig into your current business processes, including information about your customers, sales channels, suppliers, competition, marketing, sources of data, data integration requirements, pricing, geographical coverage and much more. The more minute the exploration of the details is, the better the results and recommendations you will get from the analysis.

A word of warning. Our team gets called in to fix a lot of E-Commerce messes because too little investigation was done on the integration of data between systems. The integration of your new E-Commerce site with backend business systems is often an area that gets glossed over. Big assumptions are made that turn out to be wrong and later cause timeline delays and additional budget demands. Make sure you have the technical talent within your business or from an external partner to allow accurate information gathering on the front-end and proper integration on the back-end.

Allow at least a few weeks—if not a few months—for the analysis information to be gathered, reviewed and used to develop a plan for your new E-Commerce initiative. The budget for this work will depend on its size and scope, but it's reasonable to expect to invest somewhere between $10,000 and $100,000 to get a solid plan in place that takes into consideration how new online sales will be conducted, both externally with your customers and internally with your team and systems.

In our work, the analysis includes face-to-face discussions, where it's easy to dig more deeply into topics that relate to successful E-Commerce. This is also a good opportunity to make sure there's a good fit between the executive sponsor, the E-Commerce steering committee and the team that's conducting the analysis.

Once the face-to-face discussions are complete, the analysis team will review the findings, perform research, apply best practice standards, create an initial timeline and assess the required budget to bring the plan to fruition. In some cases, the provider may also build some initial mockups or wireframes to help convey how your E-Commerce will function.

Depending on the complexity of your products and sales process, and your budget, the analysis deliverables may include a phased approach to the E-Commerce launch. This is often a great way to make progress without overstressing the team. It also provides business leaders with actual results before having to fully complete and pay for all of the planned E-Commerce features and functions.

With mockups and wireframes in hand, which visually show how an E-Commerce experience will work, an organization can explore options and changes before expensive programming or configuration work begins. Be sure to take the time to carefully review the plan and its deliverables to ensure full understanding. If questions arise, make sure those get asked and answered. It's so much easier to make adjustments at this stage than after development is underway.

Just like building a new home, you'll be in a much better position if you have high-quality blueprints at the start. E-

Commerce analysis early on is a great way to get all of the pieces of the puzzle in the right place and get your team excited about the process.

To prepare for your upcoming E-Commerce analysis, you need to first determine who is going to do the development work. If your internal team can take on this work, great. Make sure their knowledge is current, as the rules of the E-Commerce road change constantly. Even experience that's a year or two old may set you up for poor results. If your internal team doesn't have the expertise or is too busy with other priorities, you will want to pick an experienced external partner.

Regardless of who will be building or enhancing your E-Commerce site, allow for proper time to do the upfront analysis. Don't rush this process, as it can make or break your long-term digital commerce success.

Interview, in person, some analysis teams. Ask them to show you examples of their recent work and dig for details about how they've helped other departments or companies achieve their E-Commerce goals. Determine whether their experience and process are a good fit for your organization. While money is always an important consideration, analysis is an area where it can be costly to pick the cheapest option.

Section 1 – PLANNING Your E-Commerce

CHALLENGE:
Hiring an internal team or an external partner?
Hiring—let alone finding—experienced digital people is a challenge. Is it better to hire an internal digital expert or hire an external partner? We'll walk you through the options and help you decide what's best for your business.

As founders of a good-sized web development agency, we'll share our bias from the outset as we provide guidance to this challenge. We believe that companies are best served by using a qualified, digitally-focused firm to help navigate the digital waters. There is just too much for one, two or even a few people to know. The disciplines required to guide user experience, product taxonomy, data structure, data integration, programming, responsive design, SEO, ADA compliance, hosting and analytics are vast and everchanging.

Now, we know companies that are successfully approaching E-Commerce in other ways. Some choose to have a key marketing person coordinate external activities with various partners, while others hire a small team but keep their focus to a minimum number of tactics. In our practice, we've had the pleasure of working with people who really know their craft and many others who are so off-base in their understanding of the digital world that it makes us cry.

So, how should your company move forward and take advantage of online sales opportunities? Let's be practical for a minute. Depending on your level of commitment and financial situation, you may not be in a position to put this book down and start doing more than maybe one or two things. You can start the process by identifying something in this book that you think makes sense for your customers, partners or employees. Depending on what that is, you may be able to engage someone internally or hire an outside consultant to perform specific tasks.

Some of the tactics outlined in this book, like developing a large-scale E-Commerce website or strategic digital marketing campaign will require broader capabilities. For those activities, unless you have a large marketing and IT staff, you'll want to partner with a firm that has a proven track record. Find a group you'd really like to work with and one that's genuinely willing to understand your business. While it might be tempting to hire the lowest-cost firm, we strongly recommend that you select a partner based on their capabilities and experience.

If you're looking to hire an individual to help manage your company's E-Commerce efforts, we recommend finding someone that has experience with developing comprehensive E-Commerce sites—not just a marketer. The knowledge required to design, build, populate and market a world-class E-Commerce site is difficult (actually it's nearly impossible) to come by in one individual. Even an expert will need help in different areas. Building and growing E-Commerce is not a one-person job.

Interns are great and well suited to play supporting roles within your digital marketing team, but don't let them operate unsupervised or you'll risk becoming a statistic in one of our future books! While it may seem right to put an intern in charge of your company's Facebook account because they "get" social media, don't do it. Let them gain some real-world business experience by working alongside your more senior team members before handing that kind of responsibility to them.

Hiring freelancers is another option that works for some companies. The upside is that you can use these people when you need them and their fees are generally lower than an agency's. The risk is that freelancers can get busy with other client work and become unavailable to you at a time when you really need them, or they can get out of the freelance business altogether, leaving your company to fend for itself.

There's no perfect solution. You'll need to figure out what's best for your company. If you have a sufficient budget to tackle some of the larger tasks, engaging an agency of diverse skill sets will be highly desirable. If your company needs to generate small successes to support further investment, using freelancers could be a better solution. Our final caveat to using freelancers is to pick one that's located in your area. We've seen too many instances where companies were ultimately left with a mess when faraway freelancers stalled projects, became completely unavailable or, worse yet, stole programming code for use on a competitor's project.

Regardless of how you choose to move your company's E-Commerce efforts forward, we have one overarching recommendation. Pick people who understand business. The number of people who claim to be great digital experts is in the millions, for sure. The reality, though, is that while the great majority of these people may know something about how to use digital tools, they often don't understand how business really works. That's like hiring someone who knows how to drive a car but can't read a map. They make mistakes because they don't realize how the various facets of E-Commerce come together and connect to the business. Don't make the costly mistake of hiring someone who just knows a few digital tools. Take the time to hire someone (or better yet a team) that has genuine business acumen.

A final thought about hiring a freelancer or technical development agency, please refrain from using RFPs as the mechanism to hire. Interview people or firms and pick the one you like based on their personality, experience and reputation. RFPs are almost always bad because there's not enough information to provide a realistic proposal and therefore the budget you'll get back will either be too high, because the responding company is trying to protect itself from what is unknown, or the estimate will be too low because the respondent is okay winning the business and later raising the fees after the deal is struck. RFPs take too much time and effort for all parties involved. You'll be miles ahead if you'll just meet with people or firms until you find one you like.

Create an organizational chart for what your digital team should look like in the future. Then assign (only) one major competency to each individual (i.e. "data integration specialist"). If there are gaps between the expertise you need and what you currently have, detail the needed capabilities for each opening but leave the name open. You will likely end up with a chart that reflects 7 or more people.

Once you've drafted the roles and responsibilities you need, prioritize the open seats so you know which one individual is most important to your organization as you begin doing E-Commerce activities. As budget allows, assuming you want to build an internal team, make this person your first hire.

In the meantime, turn to freelancers or a technical development firm to handle the duties that are missing on your org chart. Over time you can continue to build out your team by hiring one or two people each year, or you may decide that using an external expert makes more sense for your business.

Section 1 – PLANNING Your E-Commerce

CHALLENGE:
Adding direct-to-consumer sales to a B2B model

Transitioning your company to take on at least some direct end-consumer sales opportunities could help you transform your business into a different and more profitable organization.

If your business has relied on dealers, distributors, manufacturers' reps, wholesalers or retailers to handle the marketing and sales of your products to end consumers, it can be a big hurdle to go after that business directly. Even though many of these organizations are mere order takers, making no effort to actually build a market for your products, they will often balk if they see your company trying to bypass them. This can put your sales efforts in a precarious spot.

So how do you get around this kind of complicated situation? Here are some of the things we've seen work for our clients who have faced this dilemma.

> *Sell replacement parts online.* For many intermediaries, the sale of spare parts is a real pain. There's often a lot of handholding required to determine which part or parts are needed and, typically, the order values are modest. For the manufacturer, however, the prospect of selling these parts directly can be enticing because you already have the customer service capacity and expertise available, and your margin on spare parts is often substantial. With online order-by-schematics, buyers can self-serve and quickly find the correct part(s) they need to make a repair. Often, we find that channel partners are happy to let manufacturers handle spare part orders directly. This approach can often be a win-win for all parties involved. The end customer gets the right part the first time, the sales partner doesn't have to bother with small replacement orders and the

manufacturer can generate a lot of high margin orders. During this process, the manufacturer is also able to build initial relationships directly with end customers.

Sell only specific products. In addition to replacement parts, we've seen some companies isolate a specific set of products they choose to handle directly. The reasons vary, but most often the products are complex and require engineering or other customizations to fully spec, build and fulfill. The advantage of this approach is your company's ability to test the waters and see how easy it is (or isn't) to handle direct inquiries online or over the phone. If you find this method works well, you may decide that it makes sense to expand the range of equipment offered to end customers.

Handle orders directly in areas where you don't have representation. Perhaps your business has good sales partner coverage in many but not all geographic areas. If this is your company's situation, consider selling directly into the gaps. The trick is to make sure that the customers to whom you sell are really located in the defined area and not crossing over from an existing channel partner's territory. This can be resolved by scrutinizing an order's ship-to address or by offering the products at the same price as the neighboring area dealer. You'll achieve a better margin on this business, as there's no commission to pay. Once you have built up enough sales in the gap market(s), you can decide whether to attract a worthy sales partner, giving them a nice book of business from which to start or continue to take on the business directly.

Create a direct line of products. Another approach to get into direct sales is to create a new line of products that are designed exclusively for the end consumer market. Generally, these kinds of direct-line products have fewer features and are lower priced. In this scenario, the company's original, higher quality products continue to be sold only through sales channel partners.

If your products can be built with differing levels of quality and features, selling the lower-cost versions directly to consumers could be a reasonable way to add incremental sales to your manufacturing business. We've known companies that have been very successful in deploying this approach. They especially like having the proactive ability to push for direct sales on those occasions when partner sales are slow.

Sell direct but pay your partner a commission. Regardless of whether your long-term sales strategy includes channel partners or not, you can start with an intermediate step. This concept revolves around marketing and selling your products to your end consumers, but still offering your channel partner in that geographic area commission or a "spiff" payment. This is often seen as a reasonable compromise between traditional selling partners and manufacturers. Making the commission payment to your partner becomes especially important if your equipment requires in-the-field setup or ongoing service.

The various ideas we've outlined for selling directly are viable for some companies. As you can imagine, however, anytime a manufacturer shows an interest in selling equipment to their end-users this can raise concerns for channel partners. As a business leader, you need to have an end game in mind. For some, it's simply a matter of time before the intermediaries are reduced or eliminated. For other companies, it's about finding a balance between serving their customers and keeping long-term options open. Still, other manufacturers will never eliminate their sales channel model because they rely on them to handle local maintenance needs or because they've become strong partners that consistently deliver on their promise to build market share. It really comes down to the type of equipment you make or distribute. Products that don't require support and service are ideally suited for direct-to-consumer sales. If you don't go after that business directly, at some point your competitors likely will.

From our vantage point, it's clear that in the future more and more manufacturers, distributors and retailers are going to sell products and services directly to end customers online. These organizations will sell directly because the digital world makes it easier for the connections to happen and because their end consumers actually want to buy "from the factory." If your business can migrate towards this sales approach—even if it's limited to certain products or geography— the transformation of your bottom line (and business' valuation) could be dramatic.

Create a short online survey and send it to your end consumers. If you don't have emails for the people that use your products, hopefully, you can create a direct mail piece (yes, there are still good reasons for traditional marketing) using addresses from warranty registration records.

Either as a direct question or by drawing conclusions from responses received, determine what services you could offer to your end consumer audience that would be of value to them and add incremental revenue to your business. Take these findings and craft a new trial service offering. This program might take the form of an extended warranty, subscription service for replacement parts or something completely new your customers suggest. Be open to new ideas and experiment to see what works. A few years from now your business might be providing new services and creating handsome profits from ideas you haven't yet thought about.

Section 1 – PLANNING Your E-Commerce

CHALLENGE:

Selling online to your regular customers is still E-Commerce

Selling products and services online is E-Commerce. This is true whether it's a brand new customer or a longstanding, reliable client.

There is a significant number of companies that sell products to the same customers, typically other businesses, over and over. In some cases these companies rarely, if ever, sell to a new customer. Even in these instances, E-Commerce may be worth considering.

Regular customers still need information to place common orders. They may need to know product inventory availability. Perhaps orders are shipped to different locations and they must communicate that information to your company. Occasionally a customer might have a special requirement for the equipment they regularly order. There could be a question about pricing or shipping or taxes. Your regular customer could have a new employee that doesn't know you like their predecessor.

In our business, we've created special online ordering functions, including the ability to enter orders directly from a spreadsheet or rapid ordering using only SKU numbers and quantity for companies who serve customers that order large quantities of products on a regular basis. Another possibility is a subscription or continuity order, where the same items are automatically ordered and shipped at a cadence specified by the customer.

The bottom line is that even your usual customers can benefit from the advantages of E-Commerce. Further, many buyers of equipment today are demanding an ability to buy online—even from their suppliers with whom they've worked with for decades. It's about convenience and information flow at a time that is convenient for them—not you.

Creating the ability for your customers to enter orders online is becoming standard operating procedure for many industries. This is new. Until recently, buyers were content to use whatever process their suppliers offered. This is changing rapidly. If you're not allowing customers to check inventory, view schematics for a replacement part, place orders and check order status online, your competitor may take your forever customer away. We are seeing this happen firsthand, far more today than ever before.

The same best practice E-Commerce principles apply to the one customer you know or thousands (or millions) of customers you don't yet know. Don't get caught in the trap of thinking you can get by without offering E-Commerce.

If your company serves a finite number of customers, talk to a few of your best clients to find out how they perceive your buying process. Investigate how their other suppliers offer different ways to buy from them. In our experience, we know that once a buyer is able to order online from one company, they quickly begin to dislike companies that don't allow that same kind of interaction.

Armed with the information gathered from your customers you can then determine whether it makes sense to explore E-Commerce in your company. If it doesn't now, keep an eye on this topic as younger buyers, who've used the Internet throughout their entire careers, are taking the reins and mandating the ability to buy online.

Section 1 – PLANNING Your E-Commerce

CHALLENGE:
Buy or build your new E-Commerce platform?
If you've made the decision to start or expand E-Commerce sales, the next logical question is whether to build a custom store or buy a prepackaged solution?

Deciding whether to use a productized online store or build a custom solution is critically important. The correct answer will depend on your business, so there could be reasons for either path. If you make the wrong choice, you could be headed towards added expense, loss of sales and much frustration.

How can you determine what is right for your organization? It starts with a detailed analysis of your products and how customers buy from you. Let's look at some typical scenarios to help explain how this kind of decision will impact your E-Commerce success.

The case for off-the-shelf E-Commerce solutions

You sell a small universe of products. If you sell fewer than five hundred products, a prepackaged solution might be a fit. With this kind of product count, it's relatively easy for you to maneuver a typical store engine and bring E-Commerce to life.

Your products are simple. Where a prepackaged online store makes the most sense is when the available choices, per product, are few and your products are easy to describe. This means that there aren't many, if any, attributes. Let's look at an example. Imagine your company sells clocks that are used in schools. Your biggest seller is a round clock, made of plastic, with a diameter of 12 inches and powered by a 12-volt battery. This clock's part number is 105 and represents one SKU (stock keeping unit) in your system. The customer cannot change the color, the diameter, the power source or material. The clock is what it is. If a buyer wants to order this clock, it's easy to provide a price and availability. You either have the clock in stock or you don't—and if not, hopefully, you know when it will return to inventory. There are no options that have to be determined.

Your pricing, payment options and shipping are simple. If your pricing is linear—quantity dictates price—and all customers receive the same pricing, a prebuilt solution may work well for you. If you only accept credit card payments, this makes it easier to use a pre-packaged store. If your freight charges are simple to calculate, choosing an off-the-shelf online store may work well for you. By simple, we mean that you either include the shipping into the product price or you use a consistent percentage of order value to calculate the amount you will charge the customer to get the ordered items to them.

Your orders ship complete. If you can always deliver customer orders, including all items, in a single shipment this will help you fit into the confines of most pre-built stores.

Product information is easy to access. If your company has product information that includes image(s), video(s), detailed description, technical specifications, available inventory, pricing and customer information in a database that can be easily accessed to populate your online store with information, a template store will likely work well for you.

Order information is easy to upload. If your business system has the ability to easily accept automated order information collected by your online store, that bodes well for a pre-packaged store solution.

The case for customized E-Commerce solutions

You sell a lot of different components. While many online stores have a total quantity of parts that total hundreds of items, some stores have thousands or even millions of parts. As the number of items in your online store grows, you will want to take a closer look at a custom E-Commerce solution.

Your products are complex. Contrast the school clock example with a replacement industrial valve that is available in different sizes, materials, colors and for various applications. It can be said that these products have many *attributes* from which a customer can choose. Depending on the selected attributes, the part number, pricing and availability may be different.

In our experience, the more complex your products, the more likely a customized store solution will be preferred. This doesn't mean that a pre-packaged store cannot handle complicated products, but it does mean that as the complexity of your equipment rises, so do the limitations that come with predetermined functionality.

To take this idea further, let's look at another example. Some products require *configurations* by the customer. Typically, configuring a part requires a step-by-step process of selecting intertwined elements. If you've ever bought a car, you know there can be many options from which to choose. Selecting one option might limit the availability of other options. Sometimes options are packaged together. Back to our car example, this might mean that you can only get heated seats if you buy the cold weather package that also includes a heated steering wheel and rear window defroster. Some configurations can be straightforward while others can quickly get complicated. The mandate is to make even complex shopping experiences seem easy for the online buyer to understand. This is done by building the comprehensive logic behind the scenes.

Your products fit many makes and models. If you offer parts that can be used in multiple ways on different equipment, you'll definitely want to look at a custom solution. Otherwise, the limitations of store templates may quickly cause you heartburn and force you to build an online shopping experience that underperforms because of buyer misunderstanding or frustration.

You have special site design requirements. Almost all pre-cast stores have a specific design structure within which your brand must live. You are typically limited to uploading a logo, perhaps a small image and then allowed to select a color palette for the accents. All of these design elements have to fit into the allotted design space. Truly, this is a reasonable solution for many online stores, but we've seen some clients who have unusual logos or desire a highly stylized design. If your business falls into the latter category, you will want to carefully consider a custom E-Commerce solution.

Your pricing, payment options and shipping are complicated. We've worked with many organizations that have a lot of pricing, payment and shipping complexities. Examples include the need to ship partial orders or ship from different warehouse locations. You may have a series of pricing schedules based on sales volume. Perhaps you have some products that require special shipping due to size, weight or hazardous material components. All of these complexities typically outpace packaged online store solutions.

Your product information is stored in an ERP (Enterprise Resource Planning) system or in business system silos. If your business uses an ERP to store product information, pricing, customer information and order information, this will necessitate complex integration with your E-Commerce store. If you're willing to display potentially inaccurate information online and require your team to manually enter product data and rekey order details, you may be able to get by with a lower cost store package but its not ideal.

Uploading orders and displaying order history. If you want to be able to provide your online customers with the ability to leverage special ordering functions, like spreadsheet ordering or SKU ordering, you'll need to turn to a customized E-Commerce solution. Providing order history to a customer, particularly if it is to include both online and offline orders, is likely impossible without a custom, well-integrated solution.

In our work with clients, we offer both custom and pre-packaged store solutions. More recently we've introduced a hybrid approach of a base packaged store with inherent robust functionalities with the ability to customize for specific client requirements. Whether you pick an off-the-shelf solution or a custom digital commerce solution should be completely based on your business needs. In those instances where it makes sense, the custom path—while more investment heavy—can yield far greater sales results.

To determine the right path for your business, map out the complexity of your products by answering the following:

Do you offer more than 500 product SKUs?

Do your products fit multiple equipment brands?

Does your product information, customer information, inventory and pricing information reside in a business system, like an ERP?

Are your products complex, meaning there are variables that customers can select?

Do your customers pay different prices for products based on their sales volume, geography or industry?

Do you ship partial orders?

Do you ship orders from more than one warehouse location?

Is your company especially demanding when it comes to the way in which your brand is presented?

If your answer is "no" to the above questions, a pre-packaged E-Commerce solution will likely be a good fit for your business. If, however, you answer "yes" to even one of the above questions, you will want to seriously consider a customized E-Commerce solution. If "yes" is the common answer to most or all of these questions, proceeding towards a custom solution will probably be necessary.

Section 1 – PLANNING Your E-Commerce

CHALLENGE:
Determining what your customers really want

Knowing your customers' preferences, desires and budgets are all critical factors to any business's success. This isn't anything new, but when thinking about how your customers interact with your organization or your sales channel partner, knowing how they want to engage is more important than ever. Not knowing could cost you a tremendous amount of money and goodwill.

While it is a given that you need to know your customers, we are often surprised by how little effort is made towards really understanding the people who buy and use the products a company sells. Often, most of the attention is focused on the products that an organization creates. While this is certainly an important function for any manufacturing business, understanding your end consumers—those who ultimately buy and use the products you make or distribute—is critical to successfully growing your organization.

If your team already has a strong understanding of the types of customers you serve, consider yourself fortunate. It's surprisingly rare. If you don't have a quantifiable understanding of your customers—to the point of creating personas for each—here are some guidelines to help you get started.

Categorize products/customers. Spend some time categorizing your products into their various uses. Are there different kinds of customers that use your products? If so, make a separate list for each. The differences will span demographics—old, young, professional, male, female, race; geography; income; industrial customer or retail customer; and traits like technology user—first adopter, late adopter, etc. The more refined you make your list, the more value you will derive from this effort.

Persona names. Once you have identified your customer types, put a name to each. For some this may be strange but trust us, it will help your team get into the mindset of your customers at a deeper level once they can identify them as a specific person. You might have a few customer personas or you may have many. Whatever makes sense for your organization is fine.

Understand the personas. Now that you have identified and named your personas, start noting what they do that is of interest to your business. If, for example, you manufacture mattresses, it would be important to know:

> *Are they living in a home or apartment?*

> *Where do they research purchases? Google? Friends? Manufacturer websites? Consumer websites? Magazines?*

> *What triggers their need to purchase a new mattress?*

> *Is their current mattress old?*

> *Have they recently moved into a new place?*

> *Are they upsizing?*

> *Are they dealing with back problems?*

> *Are they buying for a child?*

> *Where do they typically buy their mattresses? Department store? Furniture store? Discount Warehouse? Online?*

Getting granular. This is just a small sampling of the type of customer detail you need to be able to make smart marketing decisions, but you get the idea. Once you have this kind of information, you can quickly determine whether a specific marketing tactic is apt to make a positive impact or not. While it is unlikely that we would ever advocate the elimination of traditional advertising methods altogether, we do prefer digital marketing because of its ability to get so granular. You can advertise to target audiences that align perfectly with your personas, crafting messages that are ideal for each. Best of all, you can test and retest concepts in real-time to see what works best. Over time you keep doing more of what works and eliminate those actions that aren't performing as well.

When we talk about performance, it's often sales but it doesn't have to be. Let's change gears a bit and look at a manufacturer of industrial equipment. In this case, equipment that costs tens of thousands of dollars and involves a lengthy sales cycle. Finalizing a sale of this kind of equipment online may not be realistic today, though that may be coming in the future. Does that mean you shouldn't use E-Commerce and digital marketing to market these goods? Absolutely not. On the contrary, following the same model we described with the mattress manufacturer, you need to create personas for the buyers of your industrial equipment.

Just like the buyer of a new mattress, the industrial buyer will gather information from one or more sources. Today it's often Google or other search engines. Give interested prospects the opportunity to download a whitepaper on the benefits of using your company's equipment or an online case study that shows how the use of a specific apparatus saved one of your clients a lot of time or money. You might also offer the ability to provide information via an online RFQ call-to-action.

Once you know how your target audience's buying process works, you can generate a digital buying experience that has the right product content or applicable search engine marketing to drive ideal prospects to your products first and then to your internal team or sales partners to begin a conversation. Rather than a sale, the ROI measurement may involve conversions of online visitors to a case study download. Any portion of the sales process may be supported by online efforts.

There's no doubt that some businesses still exist outside the confines of the Internet, but this number is constantly shrinking. On still too many occasions we hear executives talk about how they just don't think their website is that important to their business. While it's remotely possible that this is true, how do you know? A great way to find out is to visit your customer service team. Ask why people are calling your business. Often, you'll hear that prospects first visited your website (which is available 24/7). If you really want to know, set up a unique 800 toll-free telephone number and place that line exclusively on your website. Then, have your customer service team track the number of calls they get to that distinct number. Even if your company doesn't sell equipment online, you will likely be surprised at how often your website plays a role in your end customer's discovery of your company and products and to their decision-making process.

There are other ways you can learn about your customers. Let's review some other methods for gathering this information.

> *Learn from your employees.* Look to your own people. Sit down with your receptionist, inside sales and customer service teams to learn the reasons people are phoning, emailing and inquiring via your website about the company. Better yet, listen to an afternoon of calls yourself. Are there consistent questions that come up time and time again? Perhaps clarifying the messaging on your website, literature or packaging can reduce call volume. Your customer service staff may also have a good list of suggestions from your customers. Encourage your team to always be open to feedback from the people that use your products. This is true for all industries and customer types. The findings you get from this exercise may lead to new products, product enhancements or completely new uses (markets) for the products you already manufacture or distribute.

Website search terms. Hopefully, you track what people type into your website's search box. This information will provide you and your marketing team with an amazing amount of insight. Repeatedly, we find that our clients learn things from this analysis, like new nomenclature, because what you call your products isn't necessarily what your customers call them. Other insights might include different spellings for your products, a need for something you don't already have or the realization that people just can't locate information about equipment that's actually on your site. In any of these cases you'll learn how to better communicate with your customers and, if the issues are addressed, will lead to greater sales, profit margins and happier web visitors.

Website analytics. Like the search box, your website analytics will provide a comprehensive amount of information about how people find and use your website, from what sites they came from and more. When set up correctly, Google Analytics and Google Tag Manager will generate incredibly valuable customer insights. But, you have to take the time to properly set up these tools and then look at this data. Either learn how to interpret the information yourself or find someone who can provide guidance on what you're seeing and how to take appropriate action to improve your company's E-Commerce experience.

Online survey. It's possible that even with well-documented customer personas you will still have questions about your end customers and their buying processes. In that case, you might want to use an online survey to ask your website visitors or current customers to share information. From our work with surveys, you'll get a far higher response rate if you limit your questions to no more than three or offer a good incentive to complete something longer. If you ask just right, you'll be surprised at the amount of great information you can get.

We can't emphasize it enough. You need to really know and document your customers to maximize the value of any marketing. This is particularly true for digital marketing. Those companies that take audience identification seriously and do it well are highly rewarded with happier customers, sales partners, internal team members and increased revenues and profit. This stuff really does work.

Find out whether Google Analytics tracking is set up on your website(s) and online store. Find someone who really understands this data and have them walk you through it to prove that it is configured properly. Also, if there is a search function on your website, ask to see what people are searching for and, importantly, what results they are receiving. Having these two sources of data is a great first step to better knowing and *understanding* your customers.

Section 1 – PLANNING Your E-Commerce

CHALLENGE:
Enhancing sales channel support
Your sales channel partners are a vital part of your business. We'll review how you can elevate your communication to these important parties and get more good business from their efforts.

This is one of the most difficult challenges we cover in this book. The relationship between supplier and dealer, representative or wholesaler runs broadly from love to hate. Some manufacturers value their sales channel partners and are willing to do whatever it takes to keep their relationship on a happy, even keel. Others view these channel partners with disdain, loathing every interaction they have with them. Unless you're ready to move exclusively to a direct-to-consumer sales and service model, we hope you have strong relationships with and are eager to support those independent businesses that are out there promoting and selling your products.

Depending on what kind of equipment you build, it is conceivable that today you may no longer need "middlemen." If that's the case, you're probably already moving in that direction. While it may be hard to purge long-term legacy relationships, the increased margins are very tempting. We can't counsel you in this book on whether it's appropriate to disintermediate your business partners, but if that's your decision you'll be excited to see what's possible when you're in control of a well-designed and well-executed E-Commerce sales model. Interestingly, today a lot more buyers prefer a direct-with-the-factory relationship.

A possible hybrid model for those who aren't ready to completely give up on all of the sales channel partners is to keep the very best and get rid of the rest. In those areas where you have good dealers, continue to fully support them. If there are areas of the country or specific industries that you want to go after directly, you will want to have supportive relationships with your dealers and wind up your online efforts to attract and convert new B2C customers.

For those organizations that are not able or interested in changing the current indirect sales process, let's look at how you can enhance your relationships with existing sales channel partners. The long-established rule that *people sell what they know* is still true. Your job is to make sure that your company is helping to educate its representatives at every turn. How? By offering easy-to-download product literature, sale sheets, product videos, specifications, customer details and more. Make sure that the dealers representing your organization have the latest information in whatever format they desire. Don't make it hard for them to get this information. After all, you want them to really know your products.

The best companies generate and deliver sales leads to their channel partners by building lead generation websites that are designed specifically for each dealer. While there's an investment in creating these websites, the return can be staggering. If you make the investment in your dealer's business, they'll be more loyal to you and they'll sell more for you.

You might cringe at this idea, but create an online forum to give your sales partners an easy ability to collaborate together. Let them ask questions of one another. You might learn some things you didn't know—and can fix. On a positive note, they can help each other by sharing success stories making your business the beneficiary of additional sales.

Creating a dealer portal is another important tool in developing and enhancing dealer relationships. These portals can save your internal support team a lot of time too. Through the portal, which requires valid login credentials, your dealers can access account information, up-to-date inventory, pricing and order status information. They can also download ads, tradeshow schedules, new product demos and other training information. Dealers can also view their accounts and access a range of meaningful dashboard reports. Make sure that your dealer portal is designed for use on smartphones and tablets, using responsive design. Your dealers will love it when they can get to accurate, relevant information anytime from anywhere.

Though the popularity of apps is waning with the widespread use of responsive websites, there are still good reasons to consider creating an app. One of the most important reasons is when your sales team or dealers are frequently at locations that have no access to the internet. Another reason for having an app is so your company is featured in the app stores. This enables your information to be accessible via an icon on a phone (rather than having to go to a browser).

Finally, if your business requires multilingual communication, make sure that you support your dealers in those markets accordingly. You'll need to balance the investment with the need, but when you offer native language information to foreign dealers and their customers, you'll typically cultivate much deeper and more successful relationships.

If you are looking for new, more digitally-centered ways to support your sales channel partners, consider one or more of the ideas offered in this challenge.

One of the biggest eye-openers here is proving there is a problem. Contact five of your dealers anonymously as a would-be buyer and request the same product details. The probability that you will get out-of-date or inconsistent information is high. If you discover this to be true this should excite you about getting started on some of the ideas listed in this challenge.

Section 1 – PLANNING Your E-Commerce

CHALLENGE:
Handling customer service in a better way

Even assuming you have a great customer service team, your end consumers and sales channel partners want more self-service options for accessing information. Let this growing group of people get what they want when they want it and you'll have a more loyal following.

While some people still like to talk to a human, a growing majority are tired of the complex phone trees that are prevalent today. These folks want to be able to self-serve their customer service issues quickly and on their own time. Let's take a look at how you can handle both of these types of people.

Looking for Interaction. For those who want to have interaction with one of your customer service representatives, add an economical online chat feature to your online store. What's great about these tools is that once trained, a customer service agent can handle multiple conversations at once. Also, because most inbound chat requests will be about similar things, it's easy to build an online database of well-written responses. This library of common answers will make it easier for your rep to handle questions and ensure consistency across your customer service team.

If you have sales channel partners who are looking for guidance or customer service and you happen to have sufficient staff, it's a good idea to establish specialized customer service reps who handle these "internal" requests for information. Make your dealers feel special by providing timely and accurate customer service and they'll buy more from you.

Another way to provide good customer service is to have your best reps respond to inbound requests from Facebook and Twitter. These social channels are becoming more popular for quick, transactional issues and for urgent matters.

Self-Service, Please. There's a growing population that hopes to never have to actually talk to anyone on your company's phone lines. They want to get online, get their issue resolved and then move on. The idea of having to stumble through a recording of your company's extensions may drive them to a competitor that offers faster online customer service. This is a big deal—and becoming more important all the time. If you don't believe us, look around the next time you're out in public. The smartphone has taken over communication and patience is in shorter supply than ever.

One way to support your customers is to offer online education and training. This is true whether you're selling to dealers or end-users. If people want to view training on how to use your product in a short video series, give them that option. They'll value your company for making it easy to get what they need. Over time, you'll have great cheerleaders for your business.

You might also consider offering your end-consumers the ability to register their warranty online. Not only can you gather the information you need to track warranty issues, but even if you don't sell equipment directly (your dealer does), you will now have the end customer's information.

Once you know your customers by name and email, you can proactively send offers on their birthday, anniversary or other desired, personalized occasions. We don't advocate alienating your sales channel partner, but you may be able to grow your business by connecting with the people who use the products you make. Building this list is one of the most valuable ways to protect your interests should your relationship with a dealer ever go awry.

If you are sending correspondence directly to your end consumers, one of the ways you can be most relevant is to segment your customers into groups and leverage that information to your benefit. Doing this will allow you to show product photos that match what your customers currently have or need. You'll validate that you understand your customer when the information you send shows imagery of their exact product in the background.

If you don't have any segmentation applied to your customer emails, then your first step is to begin that process. This can be done by running your email list through a classification program. With each new email you send, use a survey to ask a simple, easy-to-answer question. As responses come in, start dividing your list into appropriate groups. You may have to ask a series of questions over time, but once you get your lists aligned you'll be in a position to market your equipment more efficiently.

Most electronic newsletter tools will track which news article or promotion each user clicks. This information can then be used to assist in the segmentation process. With these divided lists in hand, you can provide proactive ideas for maintenance and replacement part purchasing. These tactics will help build a strong relationship with your customers. They will come to appreciate that you have their best interests in mind when every communication they receive from you is timely, relevant and helps them use your product effectively.

Even if you rely on channel partners to sell and service your equipment, you can still have a relationship with your end customers. Through regular communication with these people, you can listen to their ideas, which may generate new products, new configurations, new ways to sell and more.

Customer service models are changing as buyers are often willing to self-serve their needs. You can empower your existing customer service team with online tools to make their job easier and deliver a better experience for your customers.

Get a solid understanding of how your customer support is handled today. You may underestimate the number of emails and phone calls received in a day. The percentage of each may also surprise you. If you don't have a good grasp of this information, it should be pretty easy and painless to get.

Assuming you have this data and the volume of inquiries is a problem, installing chat software is easy and inexpensive. Be sure not to overpromise new service levels to your customers out of the gate. You don't have to offer 24/7 chat, for instance, but add this tool to your online store and monitor the interactions over the next 90 days to evaluate its long term benefit to your business.

Section 1 – PLANNING Your E-Commerce

CHALLENGE:
Keeping up with digital regulations

Doing business online is complicated. You need to be aware of some important requirements today and realize that more is coming soon. We'll share some details on compliance that you need to know.

Digital brings so many great advantages to business, but the requirements that accompany the many benefits are both important and complex. The first realization is that the digital world is in a state of constant change. If you are unwilling to invest in the necessary resources to follow and interpret new requirements and laws, then you could be in for a rough ride.

Security challenges are one of the driving forces behind the everchanging digital landscape. Because of a relative few number of people who have a desire to steal information and otherwise cause damage online, we all have to cope with new software and infrastructure changes on a consistent basis. Passwords need to be changed, web browsers are updated by their providers, data management requirements evolve and much more. Here is a review of the things you need to think about every day.

Data management. Your list of customers and the information you have about them is among your business' most valuable assets. In our work, we see too many companies that are lax about locking down access to this valuable data. Make sure that your customer information is accessible only to those people that need to see it. Don't make it easy for a bad employee to make a copy of your confidential information, only to share it with a competitor. Take the time now to manage your data appropriately and you can minimize the risks of having costly issues later. Newer software, like Microsoft's SharePoint, offers robust document security. This means that even if a confidential document is taken outside your building, only those team members who have authorization to view/use the information can open it.

Web browser changes. Until recently, it was common for web browser versions to change on a regular basis. This meant that your web team had to reconfigure your website, blogs and other online assets to work well with newer web browsers on a regular basis. Sometimes the modifications necessary were simple and other times they required a lot of work.

Security concerns have led to new browser plans that include having only one supported version at a time. This change is actually a good thing for your business because it eliminates the hassle and expense of keeping your web assets tuned for many browser versions. There are still multiple browsers available, like Chrome, Edge, Firefox and Opera, but they each have only a single, active version.

Data Privacy. If you've watched any news in the past year or two, you know that data privacy is a key concern for many. In 2018, the European Union led the way with a new, comprehensive data privacy mandate called "GDPR." This General Data Protection Regulation calls out a series of very specific requirements for storing, tracking and using personal data gathered from citizens of the European Union and the European Economic Area. Organizations that fail to comply with the requirements face substantial financial penalties.

GDPR requires that anyone with data housed within an organization's databases, be able to gather a full report of what information exists and how it has been or is being used. And, if desired, individuals can request that their entire data set be completely removed. This is far more comprehensive than accommodating an individual's request to no longer use their information in the future. This requires that any reference to the individual's personal data, historically, must be completely expunged. Obviously to accomplish this requires very detailed tracking methods that go far beyond just storing data.

California voted on a similar program called The California Consumer Privacy Act that is scheduled to take effect in January 2020. It has similar requirements to GDPR, and we believe other states will soon follow with similar laws. Potentially, organizations doing business in the United States will ultimately have to keep track of 50 different privacy policies, making data privacy a growing challenge—and expense—for sure.

Payment Card Industry ("PCI"). Compliance with credit card transaction rules is another important requirement. Hopefully, your company is not storing customer credit card information on your servers. If you are, you need to address this quickly or risk substantial liability if someone with malicious intent breaks into your company's servers. These standards were created for the protection of all transactions that involve payment cards. The compliance requirements cover the period during and after an online purchase. The rules are complex, but our basic guidance is that you *never* want to capture or store any kind of payment card information on your servers. There are payment gateways that will seamlessly handle that part of E-Commerce for your company, protecting it from the risk of data theft. If you do any online commerce, get with someone who has PCI compliancy knowledge and make sure your company is doing things correctly.

Health Insurance Portability and Accountability Act ("HIPAA"). If your business has any transactions related to health care, including employment-related health information, HIPAA may affect you. Like PCI compliance, HIPAA is designed to restrict access to an individual's health information. Like PCI, the penalties for failing to comply with HIPAA requirements can be severe, so this is certainly something to pay close attention to in your business. If you're unsure of your company's situation you may want to have an external audit performed to evaluate what you're doing today and what potential liabilities you face, so you can take prompt corrective action.

CAN-SPAM Act. If your business uses email, you need to be aware of the CAN-SPAM Act. The requirements extend beyond bulk email to all commercial email. There is a long list of rules involved in compliancy, but the main requirements are that recipients must proactively want to receive emails from you and, when they no longer wish to receive your emails, you must give them the opportunity to easily remove themselves from your company's mailing list. There are significant fines in the U.S. and even stricter rules and penalties if you send emails to individuals in Canada.

Americans with Disabilities Act ("ADA"). We find that too many organizations are unaware of the ADA laws which could extend to the Internet. When the Americans with Disabilities Act was signed into law back in 1990, the internet wasn't yet commercially available. While there are no current ADA compliance requirements for websites, it looks like they are coming. Providing equal access to your company's online content to disabled visitors, who use blind readers to listen to website content being read aloud or who are color-blind, is likely to become a legal mandate soon.

In our experience, most business leaders are still largely unaware of the ADA standards or have chosen to ignore them. Numerous companies have been sued already because of their website's lack of access to those with disabilities. Most always, these suits are settled out of court for substantial sums. New rules were scheduled to take effect in 2014, but those have been delayed.

There's still much uncertainty about what will be required and by what date, but currently, it is expected that most, if not all, organizations will be required to comply with website ADA standards sometime in the next few years. Those organizations that choose not to make the necessary site modifications could face large fines and other penalties, just like those companies that chose not to update their physical facilities back in the 1990s.

One suggestion if your online store and website are not yet ADA compliant is to add an Accessibility Policy. This policy should provide a way for disabled website visitors to connect with your company and have an alternative method to gather information about your products, job opportunities and customer service access.

To learn more about how to make your site ADA compliant (there is a lot to this), contact an experienced web development partner that has expertise in this area.

Development Platform Changes. You know that technology changes regularly. The same is true of the underlying languages that are used to develop online properties, like E-Commerce, company websites and blogs. As new security and usability standards evolve, developers need to upgrade the tools they use to build things for the web. This means that at some point all web applications will run their lifecycle. When the tools become outdated and no longer supported, you'll need to invest in upgraded technology platforms. This doesn't mean you have to rebuild a web property, though you might, depending on the significance of the changes. Just be aware that like your factory equipment, things evolve and need to be upgraded.

Just like your HR, accounting and legal matters, it's good to have experts available to help you monitor your compliance with the changing requirements involved in interacting in the online world. While there are real expenses associated with this ongoing analysis, these costs pale in comparison to the fines that can be levied against your company if you're found to be in violation of these laws.

Have a quick audit done to confirm your compliance with the various regulations outlined in this challenge. Talk to your web team and ask them to document how they're currently handling credit card transactions. If they indicate that they're storing credit card information, that's a huge red flag that you need to address. If you're conducting E-Commerce, talk to your marketing department about how they're managing your company's email lists. For example, if your organization is sending emails to Canada and there's a violation, you could risk a fine of thousands of dollars *per email sent*.

Section 1 – PLANNING Your E-Commerce

CHALLENGE:
Looking at your current marketing
Until recently, the return on your marketing investment was quantifiable only by the opinions you chose to listen to. Today, you can know for sure. Modern marketing is completely measurable. Find out what works and then do more of that. Stop wasting money on tactics that aren't bringing value.

You know the old adage, "Half of our marketing is working, we just don't know which half." This may be true, but it's terrible. If you knew that only half of your employees were working you would certainly figure out which half!

When we say traditional marketing, we are referring to TV, radio, newspapers, billboards, direct mail, tradeshows, etc. Before we discuss reallocating funds to digital tactics, which you know is coming, you should try to understand which traditional efforts are working. You can use digital to do this. For example, as often as possible use a customized URL (web address), phone number or email address on each unique marketing effort. At a minimum, do this with each marketing channel. This way you can begin to account for the source of your leads and then assign them to a marketing channel. Relying on your team to ask inbound callers about how they found your company is a hassle and rarely accurate. The sales team forgets, feels uncomfortable asking or, worse, just makes up information.

Using Google Analytics to see what your new leads are doing once they've arrived on your website will provide valuable information. When you then look at the cost per lead you can make intelligent choices about what changes to make to your marketing efforts. Another option is to simply ask. Use your social channels or email marketing to informally—or formally via survey technology—ask your customers if they read a particular trade magazine or attend a specific event to learn more about your industry.

In addition to measuring everything you can, use digital marketing to enhance your physical events, like tradeshows. You might consider placing a kiosk in your booth that gives your visitors a chance to experience your product via drawing, 3D model or simulation and then ask them to join an email list or enter a contest. The goal is to engage your prospects in some kind of tangible next step. This will help foster a relationship and get them connected to your company. A kiosk can be as simple as an iPad showing a web page. We are certainly not advocating that you abandon traditional marketing, but with the use of appropriate digital marketing, you can more accurately enhance what you're doing and gauge what's really working and what's not.

If you do determine that some facet of your traditional marketing isn't bringing desired results, reallocate those funds for some analysis and execution with digital tactics. We will cover some ideas in other chapters, but be assured that your company can purchase a lot of Google Ads with the budget you're spending on running a year's worth of ads in a lightly read trade publication or using the costs from attending that third-most important trade show of the year.

Look at your next event, trade magazine ad or any of the other traditional marketing efforts we have outlined. In your next ad, attach a unique web address and phone number (unique phone numbers are very easy to get—Google offers them). Then work with your internal team or digital partner to make certain that the proper Google Analytics tracking is in place. Establish one measurable goal for interactions from the selected marketing piece and then monitor what happens. If the results fall short, you'll have your incentive to reconsider this channel going forward.

Section 1 – PLANNING Your E-Commerce

CHALLENGE:
Finding innovative ways to pay for E-Commerce
High-quality web strategy, development and on-going support is not an inexpensive undertaking. Sometimes leaders have to fight hard for reasonable budgets. We'll share some ideas on how you may be able to find external support to help pay for your E-Commerce investments.

Budgets for developing new E-Commerce websites range from a few thousand to millions of dollars. When the analysis work is properly done on the frontend of a new initiative, it's pretty easy to build an ROI model that supports the required budget. Sometimes, however, for a variety of reasons you may find yourself with a need for E-Commerce functionalities that exceed the available budget. If you're in this situation, here are some ideas you might investigate.

We've seen these approaches work with our clients and hope they can help you get to where you need to be online if investment dollars are a problem for you.

Co-op Advertising. You may already be utilizing co-op advertising dollars to help support marketing efforts in your organization. Often, companies are reimbursed funds for print ads or tradeshow costs. Today, many of these programs also allow the budget to be allocated to web development and digital marketing activities.

Depending on how many suppliers you use, the funding available via co-op could cover your entire E-Commerce budget. Sometimes companies have strings attached to the money they're willing to offer. Those conditions can range from having a logo appear prominently to having no competitors items shown on your website/store.

We have found that often, the best way to maximize the access to these dollars is to create sponsored areas and allow each supplier to own that area of your new online store.

Let's look at an example. Imagine your company sells hardware online. For demonstration purposes, your company has multiple suppliers for ladders, workbenches, power tools and cleaning supplies. As your team is planning for your new E-Commerce store, you learn that one of the key ways in which people buy these items is by category. This means that you will have a Ladders category, a Work Bench category, a Power Tools category, etc. Each category has its own landing page. From that page, visitors can drill down to the specific products that fit their needs.

Reach out to your largest ladder supplier to let them know that you would like them to sponsor the ladder section of your new E-Commerce site. This means their logo and line of ladders will be prominently displayed. Even if competitors' products are also shown, your sponsor ladder supplier will get top billing. If one supplier isn't interested in sponsoring a section, try another. It's likely one of them will be willing to pay to have prime access to your online customers.

With today's analytics, you can share reporting each month or quarter, detailing how many visitors viewed their landing page, how many sales were generated from the ladders section and more. This gives your company the ability to place a realistic value on your supplier's investment.

Depending on your business and the number of vendors, you could easily generate enough revenue to offset your E-Commerce development and ongoing digital marketing budget.

Pay-for-Performance. There are some companies that will take on E-Commerce development with little or no upfront payment, in exchange for a per sale commission once the site launches. Typically, in these arrangements, the developer receives its fee based on a pre-established per item or per sale amount. While this kind of agreement might sound interesting, it can be difficult to find a win-win scenario. Too often it either takes too long for the developer to recoup its investment in designing and building the site or the company feels like they're paying the developer too much for the sales they're getting.

As long as the arrangement is well defined and the details are made available for both parties to inspect on a regular basis, this can be a unique way to push your company's E-Commerce forward. Just work hard to find a reasonable balance for both organizations. Otherwise, these relationships can quickly go off the rails.

Government Grants. Our team has found some federal government grants available to manufacturers that can be used for investments in E-Commerce development and digital marketing. As you might imagine, there are some requirements and stipulations, but these kinds of programs do exist.

If you're currently selling equipment, parts or services online and want to build a new E-Commerce site, create a written plan that details how the new site will achieve significant new sales. Then check with your state and local government economic development offices to see what programs they may offer.

If you can demonstrate that selling more online will allow you to add new jobs, these organizations are often willing to provide grants, loans and/or tax credits. All of which, help to reduce or eliminate your monetary investment in E-Commerce.

Section 1 – PLANNING Your E-Commerce

CHALLENGE:

When is the best time to launch new E-Commerce?

While most companies want to launch E-Commerce when it's ready, there may be reason to delay.

After building E-Commerce solutions for our clients for nearly twenty-five years, we've learned that usually there's a rush to get new online sales functions launched quickly. We certainly understand this desire but always advocate doing everything right rather than rushing to meet a launch deadline. Sometimes it even makes sense to delay the launch to allow for initial kinks—which are inevitable with any new E-Commerce experience—to be worked out before fully ramping up digital marketing.

Testing of new E-Commerce functionality should be done as the site is being configured (pre-packaged solution) or programmed (custom solution). As major sections, for example, shipping tables, are implemented close attention should be paid to testing all site functionality. Adding new components to any software can cause unintended issues with other functionality already tested and in place. Prior to launch, adequate time should be given to carefully test the new store in all web browsers and trial orders should be entered to make certain integration with ERP, accounting, freight, tax and payment systems are working as desired.

Because the decision-making process surrounding the selection of a partner to help design and build a business' new E-Commerce site often takes more time than anticipated, there's often a rush at the other end to get the site launched.

If your organization has never sold products online, launching your new site will require special attention to ensure that the major search engines find and index your offerings appropriately. Remember, you're competing with other online sites targeting the same customers as you.

If, on the other hand, your business is already doing E-Commerce, it will be important to maintain as much of the organic search engine optimization you already have in place as possible. Without getting too technical, there are ways to preserve and link content indexed by search engines from your existing store to your new store. Though it may seem counterintuitive, even when all of the proper steps have been taken to maintain your search engine content and rankings, any time a new site is launched it can take a few days to a few weeks for the search engines to completely index and re-rank your new content. This means that you could lose search engine visibility for a period of time. It is for this reason that we often advise our clients not to launch a new website or online store during their busiest seasons.

If business reasons require that a new online store be launched during a high-volume period, extra attention surrounding your SEO will be warranted for some time after the transition occurs. The E-Commerce steering committee's expectations will need to be managed during this period, so they understand that changes in a website's visibility to search engines immediately following a launch can be negative—even when all of the proper steps are taken to maximize search engine visibility. With proper tagging of content and implementation of best practice search engine optimization techniques, this downturn in metrics should be short-lived, if it occurs at all.

Regardless of when you launch your new site, you will want to make sure your new E-Commerce experience is working properly and is ready for customers to use. Don't rush to launch. If the site is not ready, create a plan of attack to get missing or broken functionality fixed and in place. Recognize, too, that an E-Commerce site is never "done." It will require continuous review and enhancements to keep up with ever-changing web technologies and online buyer demands.

Assuming you're contemplating the launch (or relaunch) of new E-Commerce functionality for your customers, take time to map out a preliminary timeline that includes analysis, configuration or development, testing, integration and content gathering.

With this rough timeline in hand, overlay your busiest sales periods of the year. How does the estimated launch date align with your busy season(s)? If the launch date falls in the midst of a busy sales cycle, you may want to consider expediting your decision-making or functionality approval processes along the way to move up the launch of your new site. Alternatively, you may want to allow more gaps in the timeline to accommodate a launch during a quieter time in your business.

Section 2
BUILDING Your E-Commerce

Section 2 – BUILDING Your E-Commerce

Now that your company has prepared for new or enhanced E-Commerce, it's time to get the heavy lifting underway. This is the time when all the planning comes together, and your new online commerce efforts come to life. The success of your digital commerce investment will come down to how well your new site is built. Make a misstep here and you'll face much frustration and potentially a lot of added expense.

In this section, we take a closer look at the steps necessary to build a new E-Commerce experience that your customers and internal team love. Building your new E-Commerce site will require careful attention to both the technical and user experience aspects of your online business. The challenges in *Building Your E-Commerce* include:

- Integrating E-Commerce with backend systems
- Getting product taxonomy right
- The importance of on-site store search
- Why attribute filtering works best for complex products
- Merchandising helps your customers pick the products you want them to buy
- Online request for quote ("RFQ")
- The power of dynamic pricing
- Capturing E-Commerce data, the right way
- Using your E-Commerce data to maximize sales

Section 2 – BUILDING Your E-Commerce

CHALLENGE:
Integrating E-Commerce with backend systems

Most larger organizations have ERP systems that manage and integrate complex business functions, like production planning, inventory, accounting and more, into a single platform. Often these are older IT systems (often referred to as legacy systems) that can be challenging when it comes to E-Commerce. Older ERP systems can limit choices and allow technology to drive your future rather than your strategic business goals. Be sure and investigate how your ERP (and other systems) will need to integrate with any new E-Commerce efforts you take on. This is an area where a lack of understanding or poor decision-making can lead to much heartburn.

If your business has mission-critical technology systems that were built back in the 1970s, 1980s or 1990s, you're not alone, but you are at risk. Organizations that rely on legacy technology to manage their day-to-day information, can face significant challenges when it comes to embracing modern E-Commerce. The hurdles are often surmountable but there will be significant effort and expense involved.

We recognize that changing an old system usually requires a large investment and can take many months or even years of planning, implementation and training. Our focus on this challenge is based on the reality that your outdated system cannot be changed in a timely manner. You need a workaround to allow your business to move forward with modern E-Commerce and other digital initiatives needed for today's successful marketing mix.

The first thing is to determine whether your legacy system is "open," meaning it can export and import data. As an example, let's imagine you have all your product data in a legacy ERP system that you want to display on your website. Let's then imagine that your old system doesn't allow any direct access to its product data. Why would it? Back in 1982, when your ERP system might have been created, your predecessors wanted a fully secure system. Websites were still many years away at that time.

So, what do you do? Clearly, you would rather not have to re-enter all your product information into the website's content management system. That is a monumental undertaking, for sure, though sometimes necessary to get your E-Commerce to work at peak performance.

If your legacy system can export product data, then your team can import the information into your online store. That said, you may need to have your ERP expert, or your experienced web development team, create "web only" data about each product for use on your website. This information, which could include longer descriptions, images and related information about products, may not currently be housed in your legacy system.

Another way you can look at this process is to imagine that your company's headquarters burned to the ground last night. We know that's a terrible thought, but for the sake of planning, it could happen. If nothing made it out of the fire, what information has your IT team backed up? And, perhaps more importantly, what information was not backed up? Knowing what data is lost will help reveal the hidden systems that exist in your business today.

Building a website is often the activity that causes your IT team to do a complete data inventory. When you think about the content you need to create a successful E-Commerce experience, you'll see that your legacy systems probably play a major role. But as you dig deeper, you may find that some of the information you wish to display on your website is stored in various "silos" throughout the departments of your business. Customer warranty information might exist in an Excel spreadsheet in your customer service department, subscriptions to your service plan might be stored in an Access database in your service department, and different pricing tiers are tied to your accounting system.

While it's possible that your legacy systems may not allow the storage of all your company's important data in one place, once you know where your critical information is housed, it could make sense to store your data within your E-Commerce site. In this way, you can reduce the likelihood that key information is stored in unknown places around your company and make sure that it gets backed up on a regular basis. In the process of consolidating much of these outlying information assets into a single, web-based E-Commerce platform may enable your IT team to discover opportunities to update some of your business processes at the same time, potentially saving you significant money.

If you have newer information management systems, they will have better ways to share and receive data from authorized web properties, like your E-Commerce store. "APIs" are modern application programming interfaces that allow the exchange of information between computer systems. Think of them as protocols that dictate how data should be set up to flow between systems so that the data finds its way to the right place within the software. Depending on the system, this can be very complex so be sure and work with an internal IT professional or experienced partner who fully understands how to do this correctly.

Tackling the flow of information through your entire organization is the first step, but it can be daunting. Consider the "sore thumb" principle and try to eliminate one silo of information. We've rarely found a company that doesn't have vital information stored on someone's desktop, laptop or tablet. It just happens.

Have your IT team perform an audit to determine where your important data is stored—and learn how easy it is or isn't to share that information between other systems. At least then you'll know what you are dealing with. You may find that your critical business information is in good shape or you may discover that you need to quickly implement aggressive changes to protect your business assets.

Section 2 – BUILDING Your E-Commerce

CHALLENGE:
Getting product taxonomy right

You have visited websites where it's difficult to follow navigation. On an E-Commerce site, navigation through the product categories can be even more confusing. Presenting a well thought out, multi-layered organization of your products is the result of an expert product taxonomy exercise.

Many website visitors use on-site search rather than a site's navigation to find products. You can thank Google for this behavior. If your prospective customers are taking this path you may wonder why organizing your products is so important. There are two reasons. First, even when a visitor follows a search-based path to products, there may be additional filtering needed. In addition, even after a would-be customer has reached a product matching their search, they may then want to "back up" and see other products in the same category. Displaying a "breadcrumb trail" on a product detail page, which is automatically built as a visitor navigates through your site, makes it easy to go back one or more levels to view other options. Second, many site visitors don't start with search and instead want some hand-holding to find the right product. These visitors will look for categories and sub-categories to allow them to "drill down" into ultimately finding their desired product.

Organizing products into categories sounds easy enough, so what's the challenge? Based on our experience working with numerous E-Commerce clients, this categorization process is more difficult than it sounds. Not all buyers think alike, so trying to come up with an organizational structure that pleases everyone can end up in a scrambled mess of overlapping versions based on the E-Commerce steering committee's input. We often see product and category groupings that just don't align properly.

A second common problem in organizing products is that even when the taxonomy (categorization) was "good" in the beginning, over time becomes "junked up" as new categories and products are added. Rather than taking the opportunity to re-examine the overall structure of an organization's products as new items are migrated to the print catalog and online store, they are too often simply shoved in where someone thinks they can fit. Repeatedly, we see E-Commerce sites (and print catalogs) start to look like a junk drawer.

A set of categories, like "Blue," "Red" and "Green" aligns well as they are all colors. Conversely, a grouping of "Red," "Blue," "Large" and "Sale" do not align. If the categorization has been like this from the beginning, it failed the first hurdle of being thought out correctly. If this categorization happened over time, it illustrates the second hurdle noted. The product taxonomy may have worked originally, but "junk" has been added without re-examination of the whole product categorization hierarchy.

When we work with clients to begin the product taxonomy discussion, we always start with a few questions:

Do you have an existing product taxonomy or categorization from catalogs, sale sheets, store signage or websites?

Have you heard about any challenges in your current product categorization from your customers, sales team or customer service department?

When was your current product taxonomy created? How often has it been reorganized, if ever?

If your company's product categorization is based on how your printed catalog is organized, what other ways might you arrange your products to offer customers different paths to find what they are seeking?

With answers to these questions, we can start to develop initial ideas around the product taxonomy that makes sense for your business. Here are the typical results we see in our work.

> In most cases, a traditional Category and Sub-Category grouping will work best. You might have categories, like "Clutch," "Electrical" and "Filters" if selling agriculture equipment parts. You will then need to break "Filters" down into its sub-categories, such as "Air," Coolant," "Exhaust" and "Hydraulic." You also must decide if a product can belong to multiple categories and sub-categories. This decision can affect how the product data should be stored.
>
> Because buyers of the same product can often think differently, it typically makes sense to offer products using a different taxonomy than just category and sub-category.
>
> Two very common product groupings we use are "By Brand" (or Manufacturer) and "By Industry" or "Application." Different companies will use different nomenclature based on their audience's terminology, but the concept is the same.
>
> > *"By Brand"* makes sense because many people are brand loyal. In some situations, there is a technical need that requires a specific OEM brand part. What becomes more difficult with Brand categorization is what to do with the sub-categories. Ideally, the sub-category should mirror the main product category and sub-category groupings, so the language can be kept consistent. If each of the brands you serve has different categories and sub-categories, then you may want

to establish a separate product taxonomy for each manufacturer. Be ready, however, for additional work. You'll also want to make certain that your E-Commerce platform can support this approach.

"By Industry" or *"By Application"* is often a missed way of categorizing products. This is a shame because people typically need to buy a part or piece of equipment based on a problem they are having. Studying Google searches and on-site store searches, we often see "problem language" being used. Someone who needs to have a hole dug often searches for "digging holes" rather than "shovel" to use a simple example. This becomes more applicable as the solution gets less obvious than a shovel. Knowing this about search, allows you to build a proper taxonomy around product usage that can lead to the same products. To continue our example, you might have "Digging a Hole" and "Planting a Tree" as two problems that can be solved with your equipment. You may also consider offering sub-categories under "Digging a Hole" that include "Digging a big hole (over 8 feet)" and "Digging a small hole (under 8 feet)." The customer can follow this line of thinking, even if they don't know what product they need to perform the task. Using this kind of taxonomy allows the visitor to be presented with products designed to solve their specific problem.

Developing a proper product taxonomy that works today and can be added to tomorrow without having to go back to the drawing board is a challenge. You need a team of analysts who think in this fashion and can properly model a business and its full product range to a hierarchy of categories and sub-categories.

While the ideas shared here will get you started, realize that this is a big task but worth the effort to get right. Your online sales engine will generate far more business when its product taxonomy is well-aligned to the different ways your customers think.

Pull out your latest print catalog or access your website. Then take a piece of paper and force yourself to write out the current hierarchy of your product categories and sub-categories you present to customers. Ask yourself and others in your organization if they like the way you've organized products and whether what worked in the past still makes sense today.

As a follow up to this exercise, talk to a few people who are unfamiliar with your business to learn what immediate questions they have as they imagine trying to locate a product using your current product taxonomy. While completing this challenge will take a bit of work, you'll likely identify some opportunities to modify or add to your current product categorization. Thereafter, you can start thinking about making modifications or a more substantial reorganization of your product taxonomy.

Section 2 – BUILDING Your E-Commerce

CHALLENGE:
The importance of on-site store search

Perhaps the most important element of a good E-Commerce experience is a quality search.

Research shows that half or more of online shoppers bypass store navigation in lieu of the search box. We can all thank Google for teaching us that trick. It's still important to develop a relevant navigational structure to make it easy for buyers to find what they're looking for, but it's equally important to set up and track a great search experience.

We've all been to websites that just seem to understand what we want. Amazon certainly is a great example of such a store. One of the key factors in creating a shopping experience that is in tune with your buyers is to get the search functionality set up correctly. First, you need to offer the ability for people to enter keywords and phrases to find what they're seeking. Depending on your product range, you may need to offer additional filters to make the search process easier to manage.

If you have a limited number of products or your products are easy to categorize, you may be able to use a basic search. This simply means that you'll have a database of products, part numbers and descriptions that can be easily accessed based on what is entered in the search box. For those of you that have many products or complex products, you'll want to look at more advanced search tools.

To illustrate what we mean by complex products, let's look at a company that sells automotive replacement parts for multiple brands. A customer seeking a replacement mirror for a 2017 Chevy Impala,, might type in any of the following into the search (and a limitless number of other options could be entered as well):

Mirror
Replacement Mirror
Impala Mirror
2017 Chevy Mirror
Chevy Impala Mirror
Mirror for Chevy Impala

In this example, if just "Mirror" is entered, your customer could easily see hundreds or even thousands of results. This is because you carry replacement mirrors for many makes and models and years. To help the visitor find what they need, you can implement search filtering. In this case, you might add a Make, Model and Year dropdown list to the search, mandating that the customer indicate the specific car upon which the mirror will be mounted.

To make a search like this work, you have to have the right data from which to pull the search results. Your products have to be organized with consistent information that can be accessed by the search programming code to retrieve those products that match the search requirements. If you're receiving part information from different suppliers, often some massaging of data will be necessary to get full and consistent information for all parts. This requires some tedious work but will make your store more user-friendly—and that means more sales.

Another consideration is getting the nomenclature right. We have a client that sells a broad range of doorknobs. At least that's what most people call them. For years, they only sold to home builders (B2B). The industry term for doorknobs is "handle sets." When this company decided to sell directly to homeowners doing remodeling work, they quickly realized that all of their product data was missing the consumer-friendly term "doorknob(s)."

Nomenclature can be an issue between different geographies or industries as well. It's just something you must be aware of in order to appropriately serve customers. As we often say, always stand in your customers' shoes as you build your new website/online store to make certain they will be able to easily find what they need.

Back to the product database, if you sell handle sets to contractors and doorknobs to homeowners, you will want to create what's called *metadata* to associate details of a product that covers all terminology used to describe it. That way, as visitors enter the words they use to describe "the thing that opens a door" into your search, they'll get to the products they want. In this case, they're the same product but called two different things by different buying audiences.

Here's an important tip that is often overlooked. Capture and review what people are entering in your site search. This will allow you to see what terms are used. This "voice of the customer" can be leveraged for site content enhancements and other marketing you may be doing. Also, make sure to have an exception report created that notifies you anytime a visitor searches on something and gets zero results. In our audit work, we regularly find instances where a company has the product people are searching for but because they don't have proper descriptions, the would-be buyer never finds the product. This is easy to fix if you keep an eye on your search results.

Getting your online store's search right is a neverending process. Keep a watchful eye on what your customers type into search and as you add new products to your store, be sure to have complete and consistent data that encompasses nomenclature used by all buyer types.

Another great way to get customers quickly to desired products is to offer attribute filtering. We'll cover this concept in the next chapter.

Section 2 – BUILDING Your E-Commerce

CHALLENGE:
Why attribute filtering works best for complex products

People shop in different ways. Some use navigation and some use keyword search. With a small number of products, either of these methods will get your customers to a digestible number of products. When you start to have hundreds or more SKUs, however, your customers may need a little help getting to just the right part or product.

One of the biggest challenges we've seen with our clients is gathering enough information about their products to make the shopping experience effective. If you are starting from scratch, you are – well – starting from scratch and will need a lot of information to bring your online store to life. If you are getting product information from an existing backend system, like an ERP or point of sale system, you likely have the product name, part number, price and other fields of data already stored.

This information is typically very clinical and is often captured IN ALL CAPS. This, by the way, is a giveaway on websites that the product data is being pulled directly from an older system. You may also ask vendor partners, if you are selling other companies' products, for additional details about their products that you can import.

The challenge is that some partners don't have this kind of information. Others can supply a data file to you, but the quality of the data may be questionable. Often the format in which you receive the information is different from each partner, making importing and combining it for consistency in your new E-Commerce store a fair amount of work.

Given the scenario described, we start with this much information about a product:

Product Name: 310 CLUTCH
Part Number: 310T14
Product Price: $149.00

After gathering more information from an external supplier about the product, we now have:

Product Name: 310 CLUTCH
Product Mfg: Big Red Company
Part Number: 310T14
Product Desc: The 310 Power Clutch from Big Red Company is a classic cross-torque clutch that fits USA Tractor models 810 through 850. This clutch can be bought individually or as a part of a kit.
Product Price: $149.00
Product Image: Clutch310.JPG

If you have completed your Product Taxonomy challenge, you have also assigned this product to a category and subcategory.

Product Name: 310 CLUTCH
Product Mfg: Big Red Company
Part Number: 310T14
Product Desc: The 310 Power Clutch from Big Red Company is a classic cross-torque clutch that fits USA Tractor models 810 through 850. This clutch can be bought individually or as a part of a kit. The 310 comes in 6-inch to 12-inch options.
Product Price: $149.00

Product Image: Clutch310.JPG
Product Category: Clutch
Product Sub-Cat: Power Clutch

At this point, you are in pretty good shape after some hard work on this one product. This kind of effort needs to be done for all of your parts and products. So why do we need to still look at more options and attribute filtering? Let's continue to look at a search for the power clutch.

Search #1:   The potential customer types in "310" or "Big Red Company"

Result: Both searches will match with "310" bringing back fewer products than "Big Red Company," but the desired product should be in the results.

Search #2:   The potential customer types in "USA 820" or "310 8 inch"

Result: While based on the description, you—as a human—would say we have a match, but the on-site search will indicate No Match. The search is looking for text and/or character matches only. The programming code behind the search does not know that "820" is a model and that "820" is between "810" and "850" when that information is buried in a block of text.

So, how do we resolve this challenge? By creating attributes that apply to a product and then offering the ability for the buyer to filter the applicable attributes. After we have attributed our product above the data will look something like this:

Product Name:	310 CLUTCH
Product Mfg:	Big Red Company
Part Number:	310T14
Product Desc:	The 310 Power Clutch from Big Red Company is a classic cross-torque clutch that fits USA Tractor models 810 through 850. This clutch can be bought individually or as a part of a kit. The 310 comes in 6-inch to 12-inch options.
Product Price:	$149.00
Product Image:	Clutch310.JPG
Product Cat:	Clutch
Product Sub-Cat:	Power Clutch
Sizes:	6-inch
	8-inch
	10-inch
	12-inch
Fits:	USA Tractor Model 810
	USA Tractor Model 820
	USA Tractor Model 840
	USA Tractor Model 850

With the additional attribute information in place, a few things can now happen, based on how your site is constructed:

A keyword search for "USA 820" will now match, assuming your keyword search tool looks at the "Fits" information.

A keyword search for "310" or "Clutch" will get the customer to this clutch and many other products if they're a fit and properly set up. Your E-Commerce site visitor will then see "attribute filtering" that provides checkboxes such as "Size" with options including 6", 8", 10" and 12" variations. In addition to the size options, "Fits" will also be displayed for models for which this

power clutch will work. As the customer clicks on each of
these options the set of results is refined until the
customer sees only the right product(s) for their specific
situation. With additional setup and the completion of
Merchandising, the results can also include additional
selections such as, "Kits" and "Related Products," which
can benefit your customer and help increase your average
order value. Merchandising is the next challenge we'll
discuss.

If you are currently selling online and you have not yet implemented attributes and attribute filtering, select one category of your popular products. Review the descriptions and product information for problems, like those outlined in this challenge.

As an example, "6-inch to 12-inch" stated in our description will NOT provide a match if someone searches for "8-inch." Once you've found a product in your inventory like this check to see if your existing E-Commerce platform supports the use of attributes. If so, do the work of attributing that one feature for that one category. A "hack," should your E-Commerce system not allow true attributing, is to call out each available size in the product description. Depending on how your online store's search works, this kind of description might result in a match to a customer's inquiry. Do some experimentation to see what's possible with your system. Happy attributing!

Section 2 – BUILDING Your E-Commerce

CHALLENGE:
Merchandising helps your customers pick the products you want them to buy
While you want your customers to find what they need, sometimes there's good reason to steer them towards products they may not know about, overstocked products or high-margin products.

Merchandising can be defined, for the purposes of E-Commerce, as simple mechanisms and strategies used to spotlight key products you want to sell. We see merchandising implemented on E-Commerce sites in the following ways:

Before they Arrive. Although not usually listed under "merchandising," what products you choose to highlight in paid search, organic listings through search engine optimization, listings on social channels and in your e-newsletters are certainly a part of merchandising. You are pointing customers to specific products you want them to see rather than sending them to your home page.

On-site Banners and Promotions. Regardless of where and how your customers arrive on your site, the most common merchandising method is the use of banners and promotional ads. These merchandising tactics are easy to create and place on the site. Depending on the work you put into this effort and the capabilities of your E-Commerce platform, the promotions may appear at the bottom of every page of your website/store or they may be contextually related to appear only on specific pages. Most websites have a large home page promotional space, that often rotates, and the ability to display additional promotions further down the page. Other site pages generally repeat these same promos at the bottom. More sophisticated marketers will create different promotions based on the section or category of the site. All of these promotional efforts are intended to engage with site visitors and drive behavior.

Merchandising Zones are made up of a strip of products along the bottom of a product detail page, labeled generally, "You might also like…". Other iterations of merchandising zones include "Top Sellers," "Also Bought," "Related Products," "New," "On Sale," etc. All of these promotions tend to work well and serve to increase Average Order Value ("AOV") or Average Cart Value ("ACV"). Increasing these metrics allows you to generate more revenue and profit while interacting with the same number of customers—and at no additional handling cost.

The main difference and complexity in setting up this kind of merchandising zone versus a basic promotion is the behind-the-scenes work required to populate the strip of products.

This is usually done in one of two ways. The first is to have the product strip generated programmatically. When built for that purpose, an E-Commerce platform can be designed to find bestsellers, new products and even "related" products and automatically display products that meet specific criteria. The advantage of this approach is that it can be deployed quickly. Once the functionality is built and tested, your site can instantly display to visitors a relevant merchandising strip of products on each of your 10,000 product pages. The challenge is that your system may struggle to accurately make the best recommendations in areas such as related products. It is for this reason that using a manual approach to merchandising zones is often preferred.

This second approach, while more labor-intensive, allows your business to customize the results. Even for a promotion covering "Best Sellers" you can decide what to display first rather than allowing the system to select an item based solely on its logic. Building manual merchandising zones does take a lot of time, especially if you have a large volume of products.

It is for this reason that we often recommend a hybrid approach where the E-Commerce platform is set up to auto-populate a strip of products, but the company can set up a manual override. Using this hybrid method gives an organization the flexibility to promote its top products and categories and, if desired, continue to build out additional promotions over time.

Custom Merchandising/Landing Pages. Sometimes there's a need to more prominently highlight a specific brand or set of products. Creating a special page that breaks the format of the rest of the site can be deployed to accomplish this goal. Much like the endcap display at a physical retail store, customers will notice when something gets special attention. This page often has additional images, videos and other content that makes the highlighted set of products shine above others. This approach is useful when your company has a specific focus or when your team does not have the time or desire to create a special area for all sets of products.

Using the merchandising methods described in this challenge, especially in combination, will allow you to highlight the products, equipment and services you most want to sell. These ideas may sound simple, but we can tell you that many organizations fail to effectively utilize these strategies. Your marketing manager can and should spend a substantial amount of time on merchandising. These approaches work and we know that customers appreciate it when companies curate and promote products that are relevant to their needs. Buyers will reward you with additional sales and think of you as an online experience that "gets them."

Visit your E-Commerce site. Look at the banner ads and other promotional areas, particularly on the home page. When were the promotions last updated? Is there an internal schedule to keep them fresh and relevant? Diving a little deeper, if you go to a Product Detail page within your current store, is there a merchandising strip of add-on or related products?

Start by updating your simple promotions and then make a plan to ask more detailed questions about how you can add or improve the merchandising zones you have the next time you speak to your E-Commerce manager or development team.

Section 2 – PLANNING Your E-Commerce

CHALLENGE:
Online Requests for Quote ("RFQs")

The beginnings of E-Commerce can be as basic as adding an RFQ form on your website. Conducting any part of a sales process online can be considered E-Commerce.

For a good percentage of companies, the idea of selling equipment in a shopping cart just doesn't make sense. This might be because there are technical facets of the buying process that require technicians or engineers to validate a customer's needs. Perhaps the manufacturing timelines, shipping methods or export documentation cannot be handled within a typical E-Commerce experience.

Digital commerce includes any part of the sales process that can be handled online. Often, this is simply the information gathering RFQ stage. We've worked with companies that allow requests for pricing and availability via their website and then all further interaction is conducted offline. Still, others move back and forth between their website and offline steps as customer specifics are meshed with the right solution.

Depending on how you sell your equipment, a basic inquiry form to solicit proposal requests can be set up. We don't advocate listing email addresses on your site for many reasons, not the least of which is that you cannot easily report on the volume—or outcomes—of a year's worth of requests using the email-only method.

In our experience, we've worked with an organization that allows back and forth rounds of online information gathering, allowing the sales representative to gather enough details to recommend the right product or service and corresponding pricing and availability.

Often we see companies begin using digital commerce by accepting online RFQs. As the internal sales and customer service teams gain confidence in working with prospective customers in this way, they often begin adding additional E-Commerce functionality. Most business logic can be replicated in an online system. Building out this kind of workflow becomes worthwhile once your customers become accustomed to working with your business electronically. It's worth experimenting with this kind of sales approach. Your customers may well be interested and, as we've stated previously, more and more people are demanding the ability to gather information and place orders without having to spend much, if any, time talking to the seller.

While in this scenario the customer cannot complete an order online, asking them for a significant level of detail during the RFP process may accomplish several things. First, it will give your sales team enough information to provide an accurate quote. If the customer simply emails their request, they may leave out information needed to fulfill their quotation inquiry. Second, asking for more complete details from a prospective customer takes effort on their part. Once the prospect has completed this task, they will feel like they've accomplished something in their mission to find the right product and price. At this point, they may be less likely to go through this same effort with your competitors.

Build an online form to accept pricing information requests about your product(s). Having this in place will give you the ability to gauge your customer's willingness to complete an online form to gather pricing details. Monitoring this approach will also allow you to calibrate the number of questions a prospect is willing to answer before going to the work of building more sophisticated E-Commerce functions.

Section 2 – PLANNING Your E-Commerce

CHALLENGE:
The Power of Dynamic Pricing
The ability to adapt to online product and service pricing to real-time market influences can generate more sales.

The airlines have been using the concept of dynamic pricing for many years. They actually call this practice "Yield Management." They sell a commodity that travelers value differently. As airplane seats are filled, the remaining seats' value typically goes up unless or until the flight time nears and a significant number of seats remain available. In this scenario, ticket prices can sometimes fall shortly before flight time, but not always. Airlines invest millions of dollars into artificial intelligence solutions to help maximize the amount of money flyers will pay for seats. As travelers, we often sit next to one flyer who paid less than our seat and another who paid more for the same kind of seat.

From an E-Commerce perspective, dynamic pricing is simply having the ability to adjust product or service prices based on real-time market conditions. What makes this possible is the data you collect over time from your buying constituents. If you have many buyers on the weekend but few during the week, you may be able to attract more customers by lowering prices in low-peak periods. There's a blend of art and science going on here because you don't want to teach your customers to buy during the week at lower prices only to stop buying on the weekend. This means that dynamic pricing doesn't work as well if it's easily tracked by your buying community.

If you've used a rideshare service, like Uber, you know that to travel from your office to the airport is generally $20. If you go later at night, when the local Uber drivers have more business taking customers from downtown to the suburbs, that same ride to the airport might cost you $30. This "surge pricing" is a form of dynamic pricing. Because there is a higher demand for service during specific times—and a finite resource (drivers)—the pricing is increased.

If a business offers a snow removal service online, it might choose to increase its fees immediately prior to or during a major blizzard. Some frown upon this kind of practice as price gouging, but if your business is offering a service with limited capacity and you begin to sellout your resources you may turn to dynamic pricing to slow the flow of business to only those willing to pay a premium price.

Using artificial intelligence and predictive analytics via specialized software tools, some companies are experimenting with E-Commerce pricing that changes based on real-time demand fluctuations. A manufacturer of food products might consider reducing unit pricing to avoid a write off spoiled product. An online shirt retailer might reduce costs if it suddenly finds itself with an unexpected oversupply. A seller of heavy equipment in one geography may have an overstock, where a temporary reduction in price can move equipment quickly to restabilize inventory levels.

Dynamic pricing is a newer development in the world of E-Commerce and our guidance is to proceed cautiously. We believe there are some interesting opportunities to experiment with this concept but do be cautious. If you choose to try dynamic pricing in your online business, use small tests to see how it works and how it is perceived. We also suggest you talk to your attorney. You want to make sure you avoid anything that could be viewed as discrimination.

Investigate whether your business has products or services that might benefit from a dynamic pricing test. If you find something to trial, keep the experiment timeline short and be sure to monitor the details of any orders that result. In this way, you can track what pricing changes work (or don't work) to drive more business using this unique methodology.

Section 2 – BUILDING Your E-Commerce

CHALLENGE:
Capturing E-Commerce data the right way

Like never before, you can watch how your customers behave in your online store and improve their experience as a result. Just make certain Google Analytics and other tools are set up correctly to make this happen.

When we talk about "website analytics" we mean the data you can accumulate about how visitors are using your site. This can include what pages they visit, where they came from, how long they spend on your site, what word or phrase they searched in Google to find you, what conversion step they performed (contact us, add to cart, completed an order, etc.) and much more.

For this reporting to work, there is a setup that needs to be done ahead of time. If not done correctly, you will be throwing away valuable data that can be used to understand your customers and improve your online store's experience. You simply cannot gather this type of insight from any other sales channel.

Analytics is a broad topic. Our goal is to highlight a few key points you and your team, internal or external, should discuss when creating or enhancing your E-Commerce site.

Google Analytics. There are other analytics tools available but Google Analytics ("GA") is by far the most prevalent. It is free to use, and over the past few years, Google has enhanced this tool into a powerful data tracking and reporting engine. We advise our clients to think long and hard before using another website analytics tool. There is little reason to do so.

Google Tag Manager. Getting in the weeds a bit, the act of putting Google Analytics on your site has changed over the years. While you can still place Google Analytics on your site without using Google Tag Manager, which allows detailed content tagging and tracking for marketing purposes, you should use this functionality. Tracking pixels and other tracking elements can be added to your site by an experienced digital marketing person, without the need for a developer, if Google Tag Manager is in use.

Google Ads and Remarketing. Using Google Ads (paid search) and a separate type of paid search called remarketing is a powerful way to drive new online sales. Remarketing involves the collection of data about your visitors. To use remarketing, Google insists that a website displays a notice explaining a business's data collection policy. There are detailed instructions on how to do this available online, but just know that this is a step you will need to take in the setup process if you intend to use Google Ads to market your website/store.

E-Commerce Tracking. There is an additional setup required in Google Analytics to track how your customers proceed through the steps of a shopping experience. If you want to know that your customers abandon their cart in Step 3 of 4 of the checkout process, you must indicate within Google Analytics how your cart process works. Again, detailed instructions can be found online, just be aware that setting up E-Commerce tracking is a required step to properly set up your analytics.

Search Tracking. As noted in a previous challenge, on-site search tracking is another tactic our team values highly. For those E-Commerce visitors that use the keyword search box to find what they want, you'll want to capture what keywords and phrases they're entering. Your shoppers may naturally use the keyword search or its use may be out of frustration when a visitor cannot find what they are seeking through your site's navigation.

Monitoring what's entered into your site's keyword search provides high-value information. This data gives you the "voice of the customer," which you may want to use to mimic on-site content and other marketing messages. You can also track their actions on the site to see if they end up viewing the products you expect them to see. You will likely be surprised at what your visitors never see. Search tracking is another strategy, like E-Commerce tracking, that requires some additional setup within Google Analytics but yields fascinating information that can be used to make your website/online store experience better.

While there are more ways to configure Google Analytics, you get the idea. Once you have set up the tracking, it is important to review the resulting data during development, before launch, immediately following launch and regularly thereafter. We recommend weekly following the launch of a new site and then at least monthly thereafter. While our team always works diligently to keep everything on track with an E-Commerce launch, there are a lot of moving parts. Checking analytics after each post-launch update is very important to identify any unexpected changes in site performance.

Once you are sure that everything in Google Analytics has been set up and configured correctly and that data is being accurately and regularly captured, we can turn our focus to reviewing and analyzing the data. There are a few key points to keep in mind when looking at website analytics data:

Analytics data will never be "complete." What we mean is that visitors logged into Google in certain ways and visitors with JavaScript and other browser configurations disabled can never be tracked in analytics. In addition, based on the timing of certain website events, some visitors and orders won't always be recorded by Google Analytics.

Don't worry. The order data will be captured by the E-Commerce site, but in some cases, Google Analytics will not track the detail of all orders. If you are comparing information for number of visits, number of sales or specific order value to your website's internal reports there are often minor differences. Don't be alarmed by these variations. They are normal and unavoidable.

Focus less on the raw numbers in Google Analytics (which may never represent 100% of the activity on your site) and instead focus on the trends. Generally, the same percentage of site visitors will go untracked in Google each month, so as long as you focus on the trendline rather than the raw numbers you should still be able to reach the right conclusions.

Remember Google Analytics displays the visitors that DID reach your website, not those that didn't make it there. Through extrapolation, you can reach some conclusions, but if you are trying to solve why people typing certain keywords words into Google did NOT reach your site, there are other tools that will help determine this more accurately than Google Analytics.

Google Analytics does provide an amazing amount of data on the visitors that it does record. Being able to see what products an individual bought and what keyword(s) led them to do so is highly valuable. Knowing what pages visitors landed on the most and how long they stayed can be used to make decisions about where to allocate your teams' valuable time and resources. Knowing from what pages visitors left your site can help you create offers that give similar future visitors one more chance to stay on that page—potentially converting them to new customers.

Website analytics is a powerful business tool. As we said, never have marketing professionals been able to understand how and why customers, as a group (not just a sample), do what they do. Make sure you have someone who knows what they're doing, inside your company or through an experienced partner, and follows all the right setup steps, focuses on the trends in reporting and uses this information to make decisions about your future E-Commerce initiatives. Using this information can also provide guidance to your other marketing efforts. Email promotions, social posts, traditional marketing content and even personal interactions with customers can benefit from knowing the customers' true interests.

Have someone who really understands how Google Analytics works do a double check that GA and Google Tag Manager are correctly set up on your E-Commerce site. If not in place already, have them added right away so that 30 days from now you will have a substantial amount of new information to explore.

Once you have Google Analytics and Google Tag Manager properly installed, have your expert walk through the reporting with you in detail. We are certain that you will come away with a new understanding of how people are interacting with your business online. We suspect you may have a number of questions for your team too.

Section 2 – BUILDING Your E-Commerce

CHALLENGE:
Using your E-Commerce data to maximize sales
Reporting of data empowers good decision-making. It is vital to discuss reporting on the front-end of any E-Commerce endeavor.

From the very beginning, our team began designing and building online systems, like E-Commerce engines. As a part of this work, reporting has always been an integral topic. From experience, we know that asking a client what information they want to track can be a struggle. This isn't because they're poor business people. On the contrary, they're incredibly talented, but the task of anticipating future data collection is rarely considered.

How we've learned to handle this in a more efficient way is to ask what *reporting* a client wants to see. In this instance, they can articulate their needs in a far more complete manner. This "reverse-gathering" of information enables us to discover what is needed in the setup of our data collection efforts to feed the desired reports.

Focusing on E-Commerce, there are a few things to consider when thinking about reports. Many of these topics will affect platform choice and how reporting is delivered.

If you are using an E-Commerce platform that is well established, such as Shopify or Magento, these suites will come with a set of pre-canned reports. You may or may not be able to configure them based on your preferences, but you can start out with a set of established reports. As with several elements of productized E-Commerce solutions, you don't have to think about some of the setup you have to with custom E-Commerce, but again you may not be able to easily modify things, like reporting, either.

If you are working with a team on a custom E-Commerce platform, reporting should be a big part of the discussion. Knowing an executive sponsor's (or E-Commerce director's) reporting goals upfront will affect what data is collected and, perhaps, how the E-Commerce site is constructed or configured. Again, you will have to work with your developer to define specific needs, but the reports can be tailored to your existing business processes and desire for data.

Google Analytics, which should be a part of any E-Commerce effort, provides a great deal of reporting. Some of these reports require setup beyond the "standard" configuration, but still a relatively small amount of work when done by an experienced GA expert. While it would be nice to have all of your reports in one place, consider what you have in Google Analytics before investing in the configuration of the E-Commerce system generated reports. It may not be worth reinventing the wheel—and maybe impossible to do so anyway—when the information is already available, outside of your E-Commerce solution.

Regardless of where the reports live or how they are created, the goal of the reporting is to let you know what is happening today and guide your decisions for tomorrow. Here are some key considerations when contemplating reporting options.

> *Dashboard style reporting* is nice to have for those that want a daily look at a glance. Dashboard charts and callouts can provide instant data on key metrics.

> *Associate your key metrics with your E-Commerce goals.* In this way, your data can be set up to indicate

their contextual status. For example, if 100 online orders today are above goal, highlight that metric in green. If 100 online orders today are below goal, that metric should be displayed in red.

Most Reports can be designed with a date filter (and other filters). A Sales Report with a date filter is better than asking for a Weekly Sales Report and a Monthly Sales Report which only gives you two time periods. A more flexible sales report with a date filter can be adjusted to any time period.

Exception Reports can be very powerful. While the reporting of the latest sales and accounts established is certainly important to monitor your online business, reports such as "products without categories" or "products without shipping information" or "searches with no results" can help you identify hot issues without the need for constant full-site checks. It is easy to assume that nothing should be broken, but in any E-Commerce site, there are many areas where something can be set up incorrectly or inadvertently missed. Exception reports can be used to alert appropriate team members of these kinds of issues.

Your primary reporting should be focused on conversion points in the E-Commerce experience and summary sales reports should display metrics from various angles. Some examples include:

- Orders (including counts and dollars)
- Abandoned carts
- Email signups
- Contact Us inquiries
- Request for Quote inquiries

- Top Selling Products
- Non-Selling Products
- Top Customers
- Top Keyword Searches
- Searches with No Results

Reporting should be a major topic of discussion. It can be difficult to define the reports needed and sometimes there can be challenges from a technical perspective to collect and process the data desired. Even with these challenges resolved, you may still face problems interpreting the reports correctly. Successful E-Commerce dictates that clear definition and ongoing refinement of reporting be an ongoing part of any online sales initiatives.

The ability to collect, process and report on digital commerce data is incredibly valuable to the business. Used correctly, this information will benefit your customers by enabling you to build a better experience for them. In turn, your business will benefit from the ability to make intelligent enhancements based on data that improves the online buying process and increases sales over the long-term.

Make a list of what E-Commerce monthly reporting you are provided today. If your business isn't currently utilizing E-Commerce, make the same list covering the reports you currently receive for offline sales. As you consider your E-Commerce goals, think about what reporting you would want to help track your progress.

It is likely that (a) the desired reporting already exists in Google Analytics, Google Tag Manager or other resource; or (b) it should not be that difficult to create the desired report going forward. Some reporting will be more challenging if your platform has not been built from the perspective of "data first," but we are confident you can find at least a new report or two that shares valuable insights that you are currently unaware of today.

Section 3
GROWING Your E-Commerce

Section 3 – GROWING Your E-Commerce

Once your organization has gone through the process of planning and building your E-Commerce, you'll be ready to accelerate online sales growth. No longer is E-Commerce just an idea or experiment, it is now an integral part of your business. By this point, you should be able to afford the necessary budget to keep your E-Commerce experience up to date as technology evolves. Equally important is receiving a suitable budget for your digital marketing activities. When properly set up and monitored, digital marketing can produce a powerful return on investment, driving new customers and increasing average order value across the board.

In this section, we take a closer look at a variety of options that are designed to get more out of your E-Commerce investment. The challenges in *Growing Your E-Commerce* include:

- Launching E-Commerce is just the beginning
- Expanding market share
- Tips to quickly boost your online sales
- Digital follow up
- Expanding into new markets
- Generating more quality leads
- Monitoring the competition
- Selling more products and services
- Adding new ways to buy
- Moving stale inventory
- Reducing costs
- Exploring international opportunities
- Humanizing your brand story
- Transitioning to the next generation

Section 3 – GROWING Your E-Commerce

CHALLENGE:
Launching E-Commerce is the beginning
Before you embark on a new E-Commerce project, it's important to recognize that E-Commerce requires continuous care and feeding.

Adding a successful E-Commerce sales channel to your business is a great way to increase sales and the value of your company. But before you invest in bringing E-Commerce to life in your organization, you need to recognize that a significant budget is required to keep up with ongoing technological advancements, customer preferences, innovations in your business and always changing E-Commerce best practices.

So what's a reasonable expectation for budgeting in the future? While you will find many opinions on this topic, for sure, we will share what we've learned along our journey that includes customers who sell between $1 thousand to more than $3,000,000 per day online.

From a site-specific perspective, a good rule of thumb is to allocate at least 50% of the first year's analysis, development, testing, launch and hosting expenses for the maintenance of your online store in years 2-4 following launch. Such maintenance includes enhancements to functionality, technical updates based on search engine algorithm changes and other modifications to the store's logic based on customer and marketing feedback. This *excludes* any marketing budget that is needed to drive traffic to the E-Commerce site.

Realistically, with the dynamic nature of E-Commerce by the fourth year, you will seriously need to consider a new online shopping experience to keep up with the changing digital landscape. If this is not feasible for your business, which candidly indicates something may be wrong with your E-Commerce activities, you can likely keep the store progressing a bit longer with a budget allocation of around 25% of the first years' expenses.

The good news is that when your business has well-engineered E-Commerce married with proper marketing, the results should make any ongoing investment easy to justify. Significant profitability from online sales makes budgeting for upkeep much easier.

Keep in mind that in addition to the financial side of the equation are the tasks needed to keep your E-Commerce flowing smoothly. Here is a sampling of the ongoing requirements of a successful E-Commerce effort:

Content upkeep. Your business isn't static. Over the course of the next few years, you may add new products or new categories of equipment. Other items on your site may become obsolete. Someone will need to oversee that your online store is in sync with your business' ongoing changes in offerings. Typically, this person has a close connection to the backend business systems in your organization.

SEO maintenance. When the major search engines change their algorithms, all online properties must make applicable modifications to keep current. Online sales are no exception. SEO changes are frequent so someone has to be knowledgeable enough to know about those changes and how they affect your E-Commerce activities.

Pricing changes. It is common for businesses to change pricing at least annually, if not more often. Sometimes, pricing modifications are made to accommodate new customers or respond to the competition. These pricing changes, which are typically managed within your ERP or other business system, must be integrated accurately with your online store.

Web browser updates. Like search engines that regularly change their internal mechanics, online browsers do the same thing. If your business doesn't keep up with these ongoing browser modifications, your site may stop working well for your visitors. It is therefore important to keep up with these updates in a timely manner and often programmatic and/or design changes will be necessary to keep your site working effectively.

Business system(s) upgrades. If your organization has backend business systems, you will likely have periodic small updates and occasional major upgrades. Any of these modifications can affect your E-Commerce system. It is therefore mandatory if your business system(s) are integrated with your website, to keep an eye on any impact caused by system upgrades and plan for timely adjustments to your E-Commerce.

Regulatory changes. Depending on the intended geography of your Commerce offerings, you may potentially face many government regulations. With recent data and privacy breaches, all indications are that new regulations affecting online interactions, including E-Commerce, are forthcoming. Your business will need to keep current with any such regulations or face potential penalties.

Responding to analytics and customer feedback. Running a successful E-Commerce program means that you actively monitor data analytics and request customer feedback. These mechanisms provide an amazing opportunity to monitor how your customers are interacting with your business. Used correctly, you can make ongoing enhancements to your online store that pay off with increased sales. You'll need experienced people to monitor and report on what the analytics mean. You'll need well-connected team members to learn what E-Commerce features and functions your customers would like to see.

Make a list of past or anticipated E-Commerce investment expenses and then apply the guidance outlined in this challenge to see what kind of budget you should allocate over the next four years. If you haven't yet started E-Commerce in your business, use your best guess to begin building out a plan for the future. Connecting the planned budget back to the established goals will ensure that everyone is on the same page and will make it easier to pay for the ongoing expenses of doing business online.

Section 3 – GROWING Your E-Commerce

CHALLENGE:
Expanding market share

Convincing buyers to shift away from competing brands can be done if you have the right messaging and tactics. Learn how companies are using digital marketing initiatives and intuitive E-Commerce to gain a higher percentage of their total market.

If you want to broaden your business to include new customers, you can pursue one (or both) of two primary paths. You can incentivize buyers away from your competition or find people who are first-time customers of the type of equipment you build or distribute. Either way, you can find solid gains from your digital efforts. Here are some examples of how our clients have expanded their market share.

> *Order something from your competitors.* Find out how your competitors are selling online. Is the process of finding a product easy? Is the check-out process straightforward or confusing? Is your competitor merchandising other products or services that expand the value of each order? How are discounts, tax and shipping detailed? What other functions do they offer their customers (like online account, order history, preferred pricing, etc.)? Knowing how your competitors are serving customers is a great way for you to begin thinking about creating competitive advantages with your own E-Commerce initiatives.

> *Focus on specific product use/application.* Marketing comes down to presenting a valid message to a prospective buyer in the right way at the right time. If you can focus an idea to a specific niche of your business, you can make the entire message seem more relevant. While it takes additional effort to do this, it can really be worth it.

Imagine a series of landing pages or microsites dedicated to specific uses of your product(s). If your customers use your products in different ways, why not segregate the information about your products accordingly? Having different showrooms to display products might be difficult and expensive in the physical world, but in the digital world, it should require far less effort and expense. The power of a relevant message will help you land more customers and help increase your market share. Prospects can be shown relevant products in your E-Commerce store that are limited to what's referenced in your marketing rather than your entire universe of products.

Try new products, product usages. If you want to have a greater percentage of the market, create new, innovative products, find additional uses for your current line or, better yet, do both! Using modern E-Commerce and digital marketing tactics makes it easier for your customers and prospects to get a clear understanding of what you offer and how to buy from you. When that happens, you'll sell more equipment and gain an expanded share of your market.

Combine products into a set. While this idea only works for some organizations, it's a great solution when there's a fit. If you make equipment that comes with many ancillary but non-required pieces, consider bundling larger sets of products into a single package or kit. This makes it easier for customers to buy your equipment and often increases your average sale value. Psychologically, people like to buy what's easiest for them to understand. If your competition makes customers jump through a bunch of hoops to make a purchase, look for ways to simplify the process. Bundling products into a set is a good way to do this. Try different combinations of equipment to see what sparks the most interest.

Experiment with a better warranty. If modifying your warranty is doable for your business, appeal to prospective customers with an enhanced warranty. This is especially valuable when the products require expensive repairs or long outages when service is necessary. Using E-Commerce merchandising to put a better warranty in front of buyers is a great way to increase inbound leads for some businesses.

Explore different pricing models. Perhaps the easiest way to increase your market share is to offer lower prices. This may not appeal to most business owners from a profitability standpoint but growing your portion of the market may mean better service contracts or a more lucrative spare parts business. In the digital world, you can adjust pricing dynamically, based on whatever criteria you choose. Maybe you want to offer lower prices to customers who are located geographically near your distribution facilities or to all customers during slow periods to keep your factory running at full capacity. Alternatively, you may want to offer lower prices to customers in areas where you have no sales channel representation. Another option is increasing pricing in those markets where the competition is lighter. The possibilities are endless, and the results can help you add new customers and increase profits. Testing different pricing and other offer options through the many online channels gives your business the ability to manipulate and measure what works best for your market quickly and easily.

Offer a Guarantee. If your company offers a generous guarantee, like a free return within a specified time—or even lifetime usage guarantee—make sure you promote that clearly to your online buyers.

Product Badging. Calling out specific products for specialized reasons is a great way to increase attention and sales. If your products are made in the USA, it's probably worth noting that in your online marketing and in your E-Commerce store. If a product is deemed as a "Best Seller," either programmatically or manually in your store, you want your online buyers to know that. One method that we've seen work well to bring attention to specific products is the use of "badging." A small badge can be designed and placed in the corner of a product description or image to highlight manufacturing origin (USA), special price, best seller, recommended and more. The key is to be selective in the use of badging, so it remains special and not something every product in your store has.

Explore a new market online before you do it for real. In the software business, it is very common for companies to produce slick marketing materials that describe software products that don't yet exist. That industry calls this practice "vaporware." The digital world provides a venue for companies to do the same kind of thing. You can display online information about products that don't yet exist. Why would you want to do this? Because you can gauge the interest of a new or enhanced product before your team ever must build it. You can also try different versions of a product to see what interests your potential buyers the most.

Growing market share always requires diligence, but with the help of common online best practices, you can test and carefully measure new ideas in specific places to affordably and quickly see what works and what doesn't.

You can gauge interest in a particular product by setting up good digital tracking. You can even set up a Google Ads campaign for a product that doesn't yet exist. Simply create a page on your website (or a separate microsite) that gives visitors an option to provide their email to receive future updates about the proposed product. You might also ask for feedback on what features and functions they would want to see in the would-be product.

At worst you might disappoint a few people hoping to find a product ready to go and at best you learn a great deal about interest in the potential product before you engage in expensive product development.

Section 3 – GROWING Your E-Commerce

CHALLENGE:
Tips to quickly boost your online sales
There are some immediate actions you can take to drive fast sales through your digital commerce channel.

While E-Commerce must be considered a marathon sales channel for your business, sometimes you need a quick boost in revenue to meet a quarterly goal or to move a higher than normal inventory. If you're in that predicament, you can deploy one or more of these tactics to get some new online orders fast.

Run a Google Ads Campaign. You can get your products in front of would-be buyers within hours—or minutes if you already have campaigns set up. Depending on your market and products, you'll want to focus on messaging that connects with customers ready to buy now rather than in the future. Preferential pricing or fast delivery are often good drivers of immediate sales.

Offer a Sitewide Promotion. Few things get your site visitors more inclined to buy now than a good promotion. For example, a Free Shipping promotion can drive prospective buyers to act in order to take advantage of the savings they'll lose if they wait. Another version of this theme is a sitewide discount. When customers can be assured that anything they add to their cart on your site within a specified period qualifies for a specific discount, they will be more inclined to buy.

Cross-Promotion. If you have a steady flow of customers that buy a product that has accessory or complementary items, make sure those addons are easy to see and buy.

This concept of cross-promotion is proven to entice new buyers and also increases average order value as buyers add more items to their cart.

Display Ads. Unlike paid search ads, display ads are image-based widgets that can be placed on other websites and linked to a desired web page. For example, if your customers turn to a specific organization for education and insights, have a display placed on that organization's website. Make sure that the ad has an appropriate "buy now" imagery and messaging that is relevant to your customers. Also, make certain to link the display ad directly to your product detail page within your E-Commerce site. Don't make the mistake of linking your ad to your home page, expecting the visitor to search for the advertised product.

Gift Wrap and/or Expedited Shipping. If you sell into the retail market, offering gift wrap or expedited shipping is an excellent way to increase sales. Many online buyers are seeking to solve a need quickly. In this case, your visitor might be shopping for a special holiday, birthday, anniversary or other occasion. Having a product gift wrapped and expedited for priority delivery helps them solve their time-sensitive problems.

Email your current list of customers with a truly special promotion. Assuming you have a good list of customer emails, send a well-crafted email showcasing a better-than-usual discount. These kinds of emails can move future buyers to act now, but be careful not to offer unusual discounts too often or you'll risk teaching your customers to buy only when you offer super discounted prices.

Email your current list of customers about a new product. Send an email detailing a new product or product line. Unlike deep discount promotions, it's always a great idea to inform your customers about new products that fit their usage profile. As noted with the display ads, make it easy for recipients to order by linking the article directly to the product detail page of your E-Commerce site.

It's good to have a prepared list of options on hand, so when you need a quick sales boost you can get a promotion or special offer out without delay.

Investigate what reasonable offers you can extend to would-be online buyers. If you need help coming up with some ideas, just jump on to your favorite websites and look at your email. This is not a unique idea. Once you've identified some possible promotions, document the details. What is the promo's time period? What, if any, are the limitations? Are there special terms and conditions or quantity maximums? Note that the more restrictions you have, the less successful your promotion will be. What is your increased revenue goal for a specific promotion?

There are limitless ways to run promotions—just make sure you thoroughly review your planned offer with others and test your offer online in a trial to make sure it works properly **before you run it live**. You don't want to end up creating an unintended mess by having your 10% discount promotion get miskeyed as a 100% discount! We've seen companies do that more than once.

Section 3 – GROWING Your E-Commerce

CHALLENGE:
Digital follow up
If you're going to play the digital game, do it right.

It's surprising how many companies miss out on easy opportunities to increase their online sales. It's not hard work but it does take discipline. Here are some examples of how to leverage digital tactics to follow up with current and prospective customers.

> *Email reminders.* If your company is running a promotion during a specific time period, be sure to remind customers of the value of the offer and the time remaining to act. Like many interactions online, you don't want to be that company that emails new offers and reminders every five minutes, but during a big promotion, a daily reminder is appropriate. Always create a link from any email *directly* to the specific online action step you want the recipient to take.

> *Abandoned cart emails.* Hopefully, you have tracking in place to identify abandoned carts. If a visitor gets to the point of actually adding items to their online shopping cart, that's a strong signal that they're interested in buying. If they leave before the checkout process is completed and thus the sale is made, you can send an email reminder to the visitor (assuming they logged in or provided an email during the checkout process), inviting them back to complete the purchase. Some companies even offer an incentive discount to get the sale. This approach works well but don't overuse it or your smart customers will

quickly learn that getting a discount on their order is as easy as starting a cart and then leaving.

Online requests for quotes, catalogs and product information. If you receive a legitimate inquiry from someone wanting help from you, by all means, address those inquiries quickly and completely. A common complaint we hear is that companies are slow to respond to requests for more information. Worse, some companies never respond. If you want to serve your customers and prospects the way they want to be treated, set up a process to expedite online inquiries. Depending on what kind of information is requested, it may mean a short email confirming that a catalog is going out in the mail today. Ideally, this same email will include a link that allows an immediate download of the PDF catalog. Other requests may necessitate a phone call or more personalized information. Regardless of the response, always over-communicate as quickly as possible to keep your prospect engaged. The more prompt you are in responding, the more likely the individual will think favorably of your business. Once you've provided information, be sure and follow up in an appropriate way. Perhaps a few days later, offer to answer any questions or even provide a modest discount if an order is placed within a specified time period.

After-the-sale follow up. Once you've sold and delivered a product or service online, don't forget to keep the new customer connection going. The best companies deliver a personalized thank you. Other opportunities to check in with new customers include a survey (about the product or customer service) or the upsell offer for an additional service. This could include a maintenance program or an additional warranty. The key is to stay in close contact with new customers to ensure they're happy with their purchase and will buy from you again in the future.

Warranty registration. Allow your end customers to enter their warranty registration details online. This is a faster way to get the data from the user of your equipment and you can eliminate the re-entry of information, as is required when postcards or other physical mailings are used. Even if you only sell through dealers or retailers, once you have an end customer's information, they can be added to your direct-to-consumer e-newsletter list.

While automating some of these follow-up processes will require more in-depth work, our suggestion is to do a simple test. For example, review the list of people who have ordered a catalog from your website in the past 30 days. If there are individuals on the list who have not received any follow-up, manually send an email with a limited time offer (discount code) on their first order and see what happens.

Section 3 – GROWING Your E-Commerce

CHALLENGE:
Expanding into new markets
If you have the capacity and a desire to grow into new markets, we'll share some ideas on how to be successful in your quest.

We are often asked by our clients to help them open new markets using online tactics. This goal can involve the expansion of sales staff and physical facilities into a new geography or adding new equipment to the existing product mix. One of the first steps you can take with digital commerce is to invest in some geographically targeted marketing that focuses on customers you would like to serve. We work with a client that manufactures a special shade cover that protects farmers from sun exposure. They knew that there was a big need for this in southern states but didn't have good distribution there. Our team created a specialized landing page for this product and bought Google Ads that only displayed to visitors in specific states in the spring, just before the hottest months of the year. Shade sales to farmers in the south grew quickly. Our client ramped up production to meet the growing demand—but he didn't do this until sales were flowing online.

In this example, we found success. What if the demand for our clients' products hadn't materialized. Would our client have been disappointed? No, because the relative cost to try this experiment paled in comparison to traditional product launches. Our client was able to test a new product concept faster and more economically than anything his company had done before.

If you want to explore a new product idea of your own, set up an appropriate digital marketing campaign to see what kind of response you get. The more complicated the product, the more time it may take to get to an answer. Just know that this kind of quick feedback is a great way to weed out possible ideas without exerting a lot of time or money.

Using common digital diagnostic tools, it's easy to determine what keywords and phrases prospective buyers are entering into the major search engines to find the types of equipment your company makes. The search terms used can often be quite different based on the geography of the buyer. Often, your end customers will surprise you in how they describe your products. Getting a handle on how they think of your products is critical to setting up your business for success online.

You may also look to engage a digital agency or conduct a competitive analysis when evaluating a new market. Once you know what other companies are already selling into the market, you will want to know how they're using digital to promote their products. The analysis should detail the various competitors' E-Commerce offerings, indicating what each is doing well and where there is vulnerability. This information is important to have if your company chooses to enter that market. Reviewing a range of available metrics, like search volumes and keyword analysis, you can quickly gather valuable insights on the competitive landscape.

Asking customers and internal team members for their ideas is another great source of product innovation opportunity. It's important that you make it easy for your customers and employees to provide feedback, and that you review it on a regular basis. Some companies offer feedback channels on their website or customer/dealer portals. Other companies choose to offer only an occasional opportunity for this kind of input to happen via social channels or a physical survey. Regardless of whether you have an open door for feedback or just want to gather this kind of information occasionally, the web offers your team the ability to capture and measure different ideas quickly and efficiently.

After the analysis work has been completed and you can confirm that your organization still has an interest in pursuing a particular market, we recommend that you turn to pay-per-click (PPC) marketing to further test the idea. Your team or your digital marketing partner can create ads in Google, Yahoo and Bing that display only when the right search terms are entered. The ad messaging should be tailored specifically to the intended buyer. If the online visitor clicks through to your ad, take them to a special page on your website or to a separate landing page that offers additional details about the selected product. If you elect to run campaigns with internal resources, make sure you have someone who knows what they're doing. Running successful PPC campaigns takes know-how or you can end up wasting a lot of money. Without strategic thinking in this area, you won't be able to obtain realistic data. When these campaigns are executed well, the feedback on whether your idea will be successful can occur quickly and without the need for a major investment.

Expanding into new geographic markets or products that aren't currently served by your company may require some additional customer service handholding. Building direct relationships with your end customers can be cultivated by your internal sales or customer service staff. If successful, this activity can quickly lead to new, high margin sales opportunities for your business.

In the past, companies may have built new facilities, relocated sales managers and rented office space to test new market opportunities. These efforts required substantial planning, considerable investment and a lengthy time period to validate the results. In today's digital world, new ideas can be vetted in a matter of days or weeks.

Pick one new market idea and then create a single landing page that provides applicable details.

Here's an example. Let's say you want to sell a new kind of combination desk/chair set to architectural firms across the country. To test the viability of this product idea, build a single landing page that has an illustration (or photo if a prototype has been built) of the new product, complete with a full description that's filled with the keywords architectural firms' purchasing managers use to talk about desks and chairs. Include specifications and preliminary pricing if you have that information.

Send an email link to your prospective architect equipment buyers. We're assuming you have such a list. If you don't you can use a Google AdWords campaign to drive traffic to this page. Be sure to include a prominent call-to-action so that interested visitors do what you want them to do (order online, request a quote, phone your customer service department, etc.) If you don't get any traction with this approach, it may be an indication that your product isn't yet viable or that your messaging needs further refinement. On the other hand, you may find new sales before you've even ramped up production!

Section 3 – GROWING Your E-Commerce

CHALLENGE:
Generating more quality leads
Your business always needs more leads. We'll give you tips on how to build a steady stream of new leads that can be automatically directed to your E-Commerce store.

One of the most common goals we hear from our clients is the desire to attract more *qualified* leads for new sales. What makes our work enjoyable, is our ability to deliver on this need—and often quickly. For most companies, generating good leads isn't overly difficult if you follow the appropriate steps. Here's a glimpse of how most companies can leverage digital marketing to generate new leads.

Content marketing. This is a straightforward approach, but very few companies do it and, fewer still, do it well. Content marketing is simply creating compelling information that is interesting to your customers and prospects. The more you write and the more your content is focused on a specific audience or situation, the more leads you will gain. Search engines love content that is targeted to niche topics. Each new article you create is another opportunity for the search engines to index your company and for would-be customers to find you. If you don't have a writer on staff, hire one full-time or on a contract basis. Good writers will build a sizable quantity of great content that will attract many buyers over time. The more your information is fine-tuned, the better the chance you will have of showing up in the organic search results when people are seeking the specific kind of products or services you offer. Providing in-content links to products you mention is a great way to drive new customers to your online store and to increase E-Commerce revenue and profits.

Focus on Search Engine Optimization ("SEO"). Too many companies leave search engine optimization out of their regular review. It's absolutely mind-boggling. You need to be reviewing how your website—and specific categories and products—appear in the major search engines. If SEO isn't a priority, you could be missing a staggering amount of potential opportunities to create a relationship with prospects. If we told you that 500 or 5000 or 50,000 people a month were in your parking lot but couldn't come in (which is really what's happening when you don't monitor and keep your SEO current), you'd surely be upset. Be passionate about SEO because it's a major driver of organic leads. If you don't have the skills internally to examine your SEO performance and make regular adjustments, hire someone who does. It's critically important to your business.

Strong calls-to-action on every page of your website. You should know that any page of your website can serve as the first page a visitor ever sees. This is because visitors who enter keywords into the search engines see results that can include any page of your E-Commerce store. Each page of your store should have one clear call-to-action. This might be an email newsletter sign up or it could be a quick trade of an email address for a whitepaper on a topic of interest to the visitor. Obviously, if the content a visitor is viewing relates to a product or service you offer, be sure and display a direct link to your store to buy the product! A call-to-action should be easy for visitors to see and perform. Don't make your visitors fill out a long-form with required fields to start a relationship with you. Begin with a name and email. You can gather additional information later.

Create whitepapers. Whitepapers are short reports, typically 3-15 pages, which detail something of value to the intended audience. Good whitepapers often have highly designed, colorful graphics that help tell a compelling story. They showcase your expertise as an organization and solver of your customers' problems. Whitepapers are a wonderful way to attract leads. If you can capture a visitor's attention with a whitepaper, you can get a relationship started.

Be a blogger. People like to follow others who have interesting information to share. Blogging gives you or your company the ability to share unlimited types of content. You may use blogs to share your industry opinions, your new product innovation process or the good things your company does to promote the local economy. Like other content opportunities, the more finite the topic, the more value you can garner.

Start a Podcast. Offer a regular podcast where a key leader in your organization facilitates the sharing of stories about how your products are helping customers and businesses find success. Have guests who can tell how great your products and services are. The more engaging you and your guests can be, the more people will download and listen in. You can even invite prospective customers to participate in a podcast. This is a great way to create new relationships that can lead to more business opportunities.

Use your social media channels effectively. While we rarely advocate the use of social media channels to blatantly promote product sales, you can build relationships with new people who may be buyers or positive influencers for your business. Create social campaigns that people want to like. In our work, we consistently see that human-interest stories win the most engagement. Over time, engagement moves people to act. This is a great way to find new business.

Offer segmented email newsletters. While many companies have large email lists, few use them well. If you have 30,000 email addresses from customers, prospects and prospective employees, work to segment your list. How? Create newsletter content that spans your various audience needs. Then, using the tools that are included with modern email blast software, move people into different segments based on which articles they click to read. Over a few e-newsletters, you can segment any list into a valuable list of prospects, customers and window shoppers.

Create a company YouTube channel. Using video is an easy way to showcase your company and the products you offer. YouTube makes it simple for companies to set up their own video libraries. You can even make the content private and accessible exclusively to those with login credentials if there is a reason to do so. In addition to telling a visual story, your public YouTube channel videos will show up as additional listings in the search engines for your business and its products. How-to videos are a great way to engage with prospects and end up with new sales.

Create ongoing digital ad campaigns. You can build online campaigns that convey specific messages to each of your audience types. For example, if you're looking to sell a piece of equipment into a niche market, tailor your message to that kind of person and run it online, where the people you want like to spend their time. Facebook even lets you set up multiple ads that run concurrently. Then, automatically, Facebook's algorithms determine which ads perform best, eliminating the rest. This powerful testing mechanism helps you determine what messaging works with your audiences for advertising, which you can then apply to your other customer communications as well. Once you find success with a group of people, you can leverage Facebook's "Lookalikes," who have similar traits to your customers.

Use remarketing. Another type of digital ad campaign is called remarketing. Remarketing is the process of following someone who has visited your E-Commerce site and then displaying a relevant ad for a product they viewed. Learning whether you should display the ad within a few minutes after visiting your online store or even days later, depends on your business. Remarketing has proven to be a powerful way for companies to gain incremental customer engagement and sales.

Use Customer Relationship Management ("CRM"). In the old days, salespeople either kept good notes or relied on their memory to track important information about their customers and prospects. With today's technologies, your sales team can easily track the details of their interactions with customers, prospects, channel partners, influencers and many others. When you connect digital marketing activities with CRM systems, you will gain a new understanding of your sales cycles. This kind of intelligence helps companies fine-tune their sales training, marketing messaging and forecasting.

Set up exclusive toll-free telephone numbers. One of the most interesting things we've discovered is how many companies disregard the web, thinking it isn't that important to them. While it is true that some companies don't need the internet to directly conduct business—that group is shrinking more and more all the time—a lot of companies just don't believe their website does much. That's where exclusive toll-free telephone numbers come in.

In our work, we've discovered on countless occasions that our clients' websites are a far more critical component of their sales process than they realize. Although it may be common, due to the nature of your business, for visitors to reach out via phone, it doesn't discredit the value of a website. If companies don't survey their callers directly, they'll never know how important their website is in the acquisition of leads.

Having specialized phone numbers makes it easy to track the quantity and types of calls your company generates from its web activities. Doing this kind of research will help you justify the investment of additional digital marketing tactics.

There are several ways in which digital marketing can help generate more high-quality leads faster than ever before. Although not all of these ideas may be appropriate for your company, we hope you are able to find at least a few that can bring value.

Leads are the lifeblood of your business' new sales opportunities. Whether you drive new leads to your E-Commerce site or hand them off to external dealers, turn to the search engines for help attracting people who want to buy your equipment. Get with someone who knows how to research Google keywords (Google is the biggest search engine, so start there) and then run a campaign that includes five or fewer keyword phrases that your prospective customers are typing into Google to find products and services like yours.

If you sell products online today, send visitors to the specific product you're promoting and track new customer sales. If you're not currently selling online, set up a separate page on your website that offers meaningful information with a strong call-to-action, a toll-free hotline and then link that page to your Google Ads. If you run your campaign correctly, you'll be surprised at the number of calls you receive—and we're confident that your sales performance will show positive results.

Section 3 – GROWING Your E-Commerce

CHALLENGE:
Monitoring the competition

Once upon a time, determining what your competitors were doing was difficult or meant a series of covert activities. In today's digital world, keeping up with your competition is easy.

In the good old days, finding out what your competitors were up to involved backroom conversations and even unlawful spying by some. In today's modern world, information about your competitors is available at the click of a mouse. Want to know about their products? No need to send someone undercover to the competitor's tradeshow booth to gather literature, it's all online. Want to know who are your competitors' customers? Check LinkedIn. Check Facebook. Check Twitter. These and other sources will help you see who your competitors are courting for new business.

Now, some of you might be saying, "Wait a minute! If this is true, why would I possibly want to embrace the digital world?" While your objection is understandable, welcome to modern business. There really are no secrets anymore. Rather than spend much time worrying about this—beyond running a prudent business—be an organization that takes advantage of this incredible array of knowledge. The vast majority of companies don't.

Let's take a closer look at how you can effectively monitor what your competitors are doing. Rather obviously, the first step is identifying your competitors. They may be down the street, across the country or on the other side of the globe. Once you have listed your competitors, you'll want to spend some time reviewing each company's website/E-Commerce store. Some of your more savvy competitors may have microsites that promote specific products or application scenarios. Make sure you evaluate how these tools are used as well.

If you don't have the competency to review an E-Commerce site from top to bottom and from front to back, engage someone who does. Over the years, some of the most exciting work our team has done involves showcasing a competitor's web ecosystem from the perspective of learning how they're marketing their products. What we look for are the areas where we can see a competitor's approach and content, including voice and tone, product taxonomy, user experience and more. This work revolves around assessing how each competitor attracts, engages and sustains customer relationships.

As you review a competitor's E-Commerce site, be sure to note what they're doing really well. Is everything being done from a best practices standpoint? Some examples include:

- Strong search engine optimization
- Appropriate navigational structure
- Easy-to-navigate product taxonomy
- High-quality search functionality
- Brand and Category product configuration
- Displaying "Bestsellers," "Those who bought this item, also bought this/these items" and "Options that go with a selected product"
- High-resolution product images (that the visitor can zoom in to see greater detail)
- Shop by Schematics, allowing a visitor to find the right parts they need from an assembly diagram
- Request for Quote (RFQ) form for complex products
- A call-to-action on every page of the site
- Displaying the phone number on every page (ever get frustrated because you can't find a company's phone number?)
- Responsive design that conforms to the type of device being used by the visitor

- Americans with Disabilities (ADA) compliance, if appropriate
- Online chat to enable fast customer service
- Easy to use dealer (retail) locator
- Appropriate links on product detail pages to reference information, such as specifications, manuals, diagrams, related parts, videos, etc.
- Links to social media channels

This is a quick list of the basics, but it's a good place to start. After reviewing your competitors' E-Commerce sites you'll want to monitor how each of these companies use social media as well. Keep in mind that as you're doing this exercise, take time to look at each company's social presence. Also, look at how their key executives leverage this communication channel. You'll likely see a wide range of usage. Some of your competitors may have social media accounts but do little with them. Others will have a strong, well-executed social media presence.

Aside from the E-Commerce site and social media efforts your competitors have in place, you can also sign up for alerts from various sources, including Google. This will allow you to see when news, press releases and other noteworthy information is published online about each competitor. Sign up your own company and key executives, too, if you haven't already done that. It's also good to know what's being said about your own team and company online.

Just like your digital commerce analytics, there are tools that can track your competitors' websites and social media performance. Get this information set up for an initial audit and then make it a regular task to recheck. Your competitor's digital activities are fluid. Your competitors may soon launch a new online store, website or social media campaign. If you want to stay ahead of your competitors, you have to review these details on a regular basis. It takes time but the information you gather can be incredibly valuable. Besides, your better competitors are watching you closely too.

Once you have a good idea of what's going on in these important areas, you can begin to determine where your competitors are vulnerable. It is within this space where you will find much opportunity to win new business and cultivate customer advocates. To make progress, you will need to look very closely at your own website(s)and E-Commerce store to assemble the same kind of audit. Be honest. Is your E-Commerce site organized for your audiences? Too many organizations set up their E-Commerce experiences using their own internal department structure. Don't do this. Think from your customers' perspectives and then build an online experience that aligns with *their* needs.

In the hundreds of meetings we've had with clients, we've heard a few ask why they should even play in the digital space if the competitors can follow everything they do. The answer is simple really. The value of playing in this world far exceeds the risks. If you want to win in business today, your customers are demanding more and more digital interaction. And, you haven't seen anything yet. The millennial generation is taking over the reins of key buying decisions. As that happens—and it's already starting—your organization will pay a big price if you're not fully invested in digital commerce.

Make sure you have Google Alerts in place that track your company, as well as your key competitors. For an immediate impact, see if any of your competition is on Twitter. If so, it's like an email list with the people's names, titles and businesses displayed. Follow 100 people who are engaged with one of your competitors and see how many follow you back. You will likely be able to gain 10, 20, or more new followers (leads) who will now see your content as well.

Section 3 – GROWING Your E-Commerce

CHALLENGE:
Selling more products and services

Most companies want to sell more of what they make and/or distribute. If your business is not fully embracing E-Commerce, you may be missing out on substantial new sales opportunities.

For some of you, this may be the most important challenge in this book. We hear this desire a lot from our new clients. If you have a good business but are finding that sales growth has become more difficult than ever, maybe it's because you're up against new competitors, more savvy marketers or, perhaps, your customers are wanting something new and different.

If you approach the process in the right way, garnering more sales by making it easier for customers to buy from you, you should find that new sales growth is certainly possible. While we don't advocate rushing into E-Commerce, from experience we know that never before have buyers wanted to buy online more than today. You can thank Amazon for that. They've trained all of us to look for the easiest way to get what we need. So take time to carefully assess the landscape of your particular market and then be ready to take action to get online sales going.

The first step is to understand your customers and competitors. More than ever before, you really need to understand your customers. You need to know what drives them, what problems they are trying to solve, how they make buying decisions and their preferred way of ordering the products and services you offer. Without this knowledge, you could end up spending a lot of money with little return. You also need to know who your competitors are and how they're approaching the market. Once you have a clear understanding of your customers, have developed personas for each customer type and the details of your specific competitive landscape, you can proceed toward success.

Let's get back to the broader concept of growing your organization's sales. We will start with your customer data and then move on to how your company handles the sales process.

You may not realize it, but the most valuable asset your company has is your customer list. In the event of a physical disaster to your facilities, you can always rebuild. Should all of your employees walk out this afternoon, it would surely be painful, but you could rehire and get back up and running. Without your list of customers, however, you'd really be starting over at square one.

Taking this a bit further, do you have a complete and accurate email list of all of your customers? If you don't sell products directly to consumers, we'll share some ideas about how you can begin building a list of end-consumers. With this list, you can start building a relationship with the people who have the potential to bring your business a significant amount of benefit. Assuming that you do sell your equipment directly to consumers, here are some thoughts about increasing sales.

Send relevant email newsletters. Email is still a powerful method to connect with your current and prospective customers. Too often, we see companies misusing this great communication tool. Unless your business builds and distributes its equipment to one type of customer only, don't send the same email content to your entire list. Segment your email lists into groups of customer types. Then, create content that's relevant for each group. This way your newsletters will be desirable and read, as the content is worthwhile to the recipient. Another strong caveat is to use an appropriate cadence of e-newsletters that matches your constituents' preferences.

Manage your email lists. Managing the lists, building the groups and writing the content may seem like a big job— and it is—but when done correctly, the results can be fantastic. You'll have happier, more loyal customers who look forward to hearing from you, buy more products and are more willing to share their satisfaction with others. Be careful that you don't over send email communications to your lists. If you do, you'll find that a lot of good people become fatigued and will ask to be removed from your list. We see this happen all the time with companies that send too many emails. Don't be the company that loses email addresses faster than you acquire them.

There are several good email marketing software options and most offer similar features. Any of these software companies will offer a free, online demonstration if asked. Find a tool you like and then get your e-newsletters segmented and on a regular schedule.

Make sure you have strong calls-to-action on your E-Commerce website. Here's a place where many websites fail to deliver. A call-to-action is a prominent next step that you want your online visitors to take. Typically, it's either buying a product (or set of products) or phoning in a request to the appropriate department of your company (or sales channel partner). The key to success with any call-to-action is limiting each page of your website to *one.* Make sure that every page of your website has an appropriate call-to-action because with search engine traffic *any page of your website can serve as the first page a visitor sees.* Use a separate web-only phone number to effectively track how your website is serving your sales efforts.

Improve the taxonomy of your web assets. Taxonomy is a fancy word meaning how information on a website is organized, described and displayed. If the idea of getting this done correctly sounds simple, it isn't. The process involved in making this happen is both challenging and one of the most important things a company can do to improve its E-Commerce success. Whether you're selling products online or working to attract inquiries through your online channels, you either need to have a user experience expert on your team or outsource this effort to a digital agency partner. Doing the research and building a proper taxonomy requires a substantial budget but it's well worth it. The deliverables from this work can be used to inform all your sales and marketing efforts. When good taxonomy is in place, you're guaranteed to sell more online.

Create microsites and landing pages. Somehow, most business leaders seem to think that they can only have one public-facing website. In the battle for online eyeballs, nothing could be further from the truth. Yes, it's reasonable to have a primary gateway website that shares your overall brand story but having specialized web assets, like E-Commerce stores, microsites and landing pages, is a smart way to attract more ideal customers. E-Commerce functions can be integrated into a primary company website or they can be established in a standalone site. Microsites are small websites focused on a specific topic, such as an audience, set of products or solution scenarios. A landing page is a single web page that covers a specific topic.

Imagine your company builds a line of great tires, designed to fit all types of vehicles. A microsite or landing page gets your company associated with the people that use your tires for each specific purpose. One microsite might cover weekend farmers who have small and medium-sized tractors and occasionally need replacement tires. A landing page could be created that provides information about a specific tire you make that's perfect for winter operations.

The primary advantage of these niche websites is a better user experience because, in the example given, the visitor doesn't have to navigate through all of the different types of tires you make, they're able to see highly relevant information that's specific to their needs. The imagery, products, voice and tone should all be perfectly matched to this audience. Another big advantage is that the search engines will view and rate this kind of focused content higher when a visitor searches for things like "winter tires for my garden tractor."

Sell into new markets. Another great idea for increasing sales is exploring new geographical markets. One of the unique advantages of online commerce is that it offers the potential to open your business to the world. If you've always sold your equipment into a single regional area, there may be opportunities to expand to new places in the country (or globe) that have the same kind of climate, industry or demographics that your products serve. Digital marketing can be laser-focused on highly targeted areas. Because of this, your trial investment in this kind of campaign can be relatively modest. Far less expensive than building a new physical location. Try a few initiatives for three to six months and then, based on your findings, push ahead with what works best.

A/B testing of offers and messaging. The internet provides a great environment to test your organization's messaging and offers. As a small example, Facebook lets businesses set up multiple advertisements within a campaign. The variables can include color scheme, font, message content, promotional offer, imagery and more. Facebook's algorithm then tracks which ads perform best. During a campaign, the most successful ads—those with the highest conversion—are then run more and more. This kind of real-time efficiency is only possible with digital marketing and it's incredibly powerful for increasing sales opportunities.

Increase the value of each order. If your business is involved in E-Commerce, one of the easiest ways to increase overall sales is adding incrementally to each order. Your grocery store has been doing this for more than a century. They place highly desirable impulse goodies in the checkout line. You can do this same kind of merchandising online. Using cross-sell and up-sell techniques, you can get a percentage of your customers to add additional items to their cart. The process of promoting related products or services can be done in various steps of your E-Commerce process. The actual routines involved in making online add-on recommendations can be created using automated or manual methods. Related accessory items, special discounts on higher quantities, free shipping and free maintenance can all be offered during the shopping process—at checkout or even after the checkout process. When done appropriately for your products and audience, you should see measurable increases in your per order transaction values.

Experiment with pricing. If you have any flexibility in the pricing of your products, you can use online commerce to test how changes in pricing, packaging or delivery options are received by your customers. This dynamic approach gives you the ability to tailor pricing to external factors, like supply, weather and more. Test your trial prices with a small group to see how they respond before making any widespread changes. Often bundling products together can help you sell more while making it easier for your customers to buy what they need. Other companies find success in selling continuity programs, where customers sign up to receive regular shipments of necessary replacement parts and supplies. Another usage for continuity programs is having customers sign up for monthly shipments of items that typically come from your stale inventory. You make the value proposition high because the customer is likely getting a lot of value for their subscription fee, but you're clearing out your shelves of dusty stuff that you're close to writing off anyway. This kind of sales concept only works within some industries, but using E-Commerce allows your marketing team to get creative.

Consider selling some of your equipment on Amazon, eBay, Facebook Marketplace and Google Shopping. Though certainly not for every business, many organizations are finding that these large, aggregate online centers do enable an expansion of sales. There are some things, however, that you need to know before you go down this path. For one, we've seen that there can sometimes be issues with supplier loyalty on the part of these big players. They'll promote your products for as long as people are buying. If orders slow down or a competitor shows up with something better or less expensive, your products can be taken out of the mix with little notice. Another possible concern is that if your product sells well, over time these online sales channels may find a competitor to build the products you sell at a lower cost, potentially cutting out your business altogether. Be aware that price is often the key driving factor for many of these online selling behemoths. If your equipment is the least expensive in the category, this shouldn't be an issue. If you're not the least expensive, you may find that it's sometimes tough to get many orders. Finally, selling through these channels can be expensive and time-consuming. Though not ideal for all businesses, selling products via these E-Commerce supersites can dramatically boost sales for some companies.

Sell spare parts online. Many of our clients have strong dealer and distributor sales relationships, so selling assembled products directly to consumers is a no-go for them. Some of these manufacturers have found, however, that these sales partners have little interest in handling "small" spare part orders. These orders typically require a lot of handholding for a relatively modest order value. Then there's order processing, warehousing of the inbound shipment of parts and the handoff to the customer. It's often just not worth the hassle. This is great news for you if you're willing and able to try this approach. Your margin on selling replacement parts directly to the end consumer should be high. Your team really knows the intricacies of your products and should be able to quickly handle requests and provide accurate replacement part information. Shipping these parts orders directly to the customer saves time for everyone involved. It's also worth noting that by handling these replacement part orders, your company will be able to collect valuable end-user information and hopefully provide better customer service than your sales channel partners.

Sell into non-represented markets. Another option you might consider is selling your products into areas where you don't currently have representation. If your organization works with sales channel partners, you may have some gaps in coverage. Using targeted digital marketing tied to E-Commerce can enable your company to be laser-focused geographically. This means that you can garner a high margin on direct sales opportunities when executed effectively. One of our clients was able to add more than ten percent of incremental high margin sales to their top line through this one technique alone.

Build social relationships. Social media gets a bad rap from a lot of business owners who think social means posting trivial pictures of mundane activities. While some organizations use the social channels in this way, there are some great ways to leverage these platforms to engage with new customers (and prospective dealers, vendors and employees). Social media, when used as a listening channel, gives you and your team valuable insights on how people view your brand. Social media also allows you to display the human side of your business—your collective personality. Showcase any volunteering or charitable work your team does in the communities you operate. You don't have to try and sell anything on social channels for them to be a powerful sales tool. Build brand loyalty by displaying that you're more than just a maker or seller of things.

We're not saying that all of these tactics are appropriate for all businesses, but it's likely that your company can take advantage of one or more of these techniques to generate additional sales. The key is to measure everything and be ready to pivot as you learn what works best for your business.

If you're looking to add new sales quickly and are able to invest a minimum of $3,000 each month for the next three months, your go-to action is a Google Ads campaign. If you take the time to perform some research upfront, you'll get better results from your investment. We know that sometimes you may not have the time to wait. In that case, our guidance is to limit the campaign to a select geographic market or a refined product or customer niche within your market, and then go after only five or fewer keywords.

With your jumpstart Google Ads campaign, it's imperative that you get the ad messaging aligned to your target audience, otherwise, you will end up wasting too much of your Google budget on the wrong people. With the right message in place, you need to point visitors to the relevant product(s) in your E-Commerce site that offers a detailed description, high-resolution images and competitive pricing. Make sure that wherever you send these Google visitors, there's a clear call-to-action for them to buy or an easy method to get more information. Let your visitors choose what action to take but give them a limited choice.

If you follow this approach you should get positive results. One important point is that when the inbound inquiries come, your sales or customer service team needs to respond quickly. Often, we find that companies don't get around to sales inquiries until days later. This is not acceptable with today's online commerce expectations. Visitors expect a fast response. If they don't get it from your organization, they may well end up at a competitor that embraces prompt service. If you follow this guidance, we suspect within three months you will have some good new sales to celebrate.

Section 3 – GROWING Your E-Commerce

CHALLENGE:
Adding new ways to buy your products and services

Offering your customers new ways to buy your products and services is a worthwhile endeavor. A subscription model, for instance, might incentivize your customers to buy your products on a more consistent basis, giving you better visibility of your production needs. Let's look at how you might revolutionize your business model in this way.

Changing your business model goes beyond just digital execution, of course. But the Internet can help you and your team research, test and launch new ideas. While you may already have some big plans of your own, we want to share with you what our clients have learned during our partnerships over nearly 25 years.

Consider offering your equipment on a lease versus purchase basis. If you limit your equipment purchase transactions to just selling equipment, you might consider leasing to provide a more appealing option to some of your customers. Having leases in place makes it easier for your sales team to schedule new, replacement equipment when the lease term ends. Leasing also offers convenience to your customers and, often, greater profit margins to your business. Good E-Commerce experiences inform online buyers of the available payment options and advantages of each.

Consider creating quarterly or annual reports of data available for subscription purchase. If your company gathers demographic information about your customers and how they use your products, you might be able to sell this data. For example, you know that a specific type of equipment needs replacement parts, maintenance and other ancillary inputs to run well. This kind of aggregate data, including timing and product purchase details, could be very valuable to allied and non-competitive companies. Offering this data report as a subscription could lead to a new revenue stream or perhaps even a separate business.

Send monthly packages to your end consumers. If your business regularly has excess products in inventory that need to be moved, one idea you might consider is creating a subscription-based continuity program, where customers receive a shipment of items from your company each month. This approach can also be used to send sample prototype products to interested customers. This same continuity model can be used for sending replacement parts that are needed on a regular basis. If your customers need new parts every week, month or quarter, consider a continuity maintenance program that automatically ships and invoices the parts on a predefined schedule. For those businesses that can make this kind of arrangement work, it will provide a great outlet to move inventory, create a recurring revenue stream and build a stronger bond between the end consumer and supplier.

Non-competitive allies. An alternative you might consider is partnering with non-competitive allies to offer special discounts on products and services to your collective group of customers. Teaming up with other companies can lead to better discounts and better service for everyone involved. An E-Commerce website can be created to maintain the list of available product and service discounts that qualified customers can access with their login credentials.

Another version of this model is creating a trusted arrangement, in which organizations within a close network agree to combine purchases of raw materials to gain lower pricing for each business. Again, an E-Commerce site can be created to gather, track and fulfill purchase requests.

These ideas aren't applicable to every organization, but we want to share some ideas that have worked for companies that have transformed their business models. For some organizations, the risks associated with even trying these ideas may seem too great. Opportunity costs and research expenses are just two of the many risks you'll face if you attempt these ideas. This is where going online can help.

By first doing online research and then reaching out to your consumers via social media or email you can assess the potential need and opportunity for any of these ideas. This is far less expensive than using traditional focus group studies. This initial research can also be performed more quickly today than ever before. If one of the transformational ideas we've offered or one of your own ideas appears to have merit, start by creating a microsite or landing page that details the new concept to your audience(s). Then use digital marketing to make your target customers aware of your new product or service and drive them to your new microsite and offer relevant information and a clear call-to-action.

These ideas for adding a subscription model to your business can all leverage digital marketing to quickly determine whether there's viability for your company. Don't forget that implementing any of these concepts might not have been possible in the past, but with digital tactics, it's now easier to create an online store and to market and manage memberships and subscriptions.

Today, you can test and promote ideas and manage the entire process affordably. You don't need to print membership kits or set up physical stores in locations across the country. In the past, these barriers kept innovative ideas like these on a napkin, but now your company can consider and test new sales experiments quickly and easily, knowing that any one of them could transform your business.

Take one of the ideas that you believe might work for your business and flesh it out. Head to Google and search for your idea. See if another company is already offering the product or service you're contemplating. You can then decide whether to take a chance and put your idea on your company's social media channel to garner traction with followers.

Sure, one of your competitors may see your new idea, but they will likely let all the barriers stop them from mimicking it. Unlike your competitors, you will know if your new idea has the potential to be a hit.

Section 3 – GROWING Your E-Commerce

CHALLENGE:
Moving stale inventory

If you have old or extra inventory taking up precious space, move it and make a nice profit.

In our work, we find a lot of companies that have a stockpile of old inventory collecting dust. It may still be on the books as an asset, but everyone knows that its real value is pretty minimal. You may need to hold on to this inventory to meet the occasional needs of customers with older equipment. If so, that's simply the cost of doing business. If you'd rather find a way to move these items and make some money in the process, we have some ideas you can consider.

An initial question is determining who might want the old inventory you have? Is this old inventory useful only to the people who own your products? If so, perhaps you can notify your dealers of a specially priced set of inventory, available on a first-come, first-served basis. You can go direct-to-consumer by offering a clearance sale on your website. The cost of carrying inventory over a long time might mean it makes sense to offer substantially discounted prices for these items. Remember, the likelihood of selling your old parts and pieces will increase exponentially if you have a well-written description for each item and accompany the words with clear, zoomable photos. If there are other uses for these items, be sure and write descriptions for those as well. You can also turn to sites like eBay and Facebook to move these kinds of products.

Another option for selling stale—or overstocked—inventory is to bundle products together. Instead of selling one or two of the items at a time, try packaging 50 or 100 in a set. Offer a good price and you may be able to reclaim valuable shelf space.

One of our favorite ways to move old inventory is by creating a continuity program. If your buyers need these items on a regular basis or if you have enough products that are different but valuable, try selling a subscription that gives buyers a package of these goodies, delivered once a month or quarter.

Different types of inventory can dictate unique ideas for getting products out the door. Hopefully, you can use one of these approaches to get that old stuff paid for and off your hands.

Stop stalling. If you have old inventory sitting around your warehouse, go take some pictures and put a listing on eBay, maybe two. One listing could cover a small number of products and the other could show the entire lot. Think about the words or phrases a prospective buyer would type into Google to get to your products and then be sure to include those in your description.

Remember, you only need one person in the whole world to be searching for what you have. People are looking for obscure things every minute of every day. Similarly, if you have a segmented email list with a group that could be interested in your overstock, don't overthink it. Send them a quick email and let them know you are open to "best offer" bids and see what happens.

Section 3 – GROWING Your E-Commerce

CHALLENGE:
Reducing costs

Most businesses at some point look to reduce costs. The really successful businesses make this a priority all the time. If you're interested in shaving costs, you'll appreciate this look at how digital initiatives can drive results in this area.

Using digital in your business will require an investment but the payoff can be substantial. There are numerous ways in which E-Commerce stores, dealer portals and digital marketing can make your business more efficient. Best of all, everything can be measured to enable a realistic return on investment ("ROI") calculations.

As we always tell our clients, we don't advocate that technology should replace people, but that with technology your team and constituents can perform better and do more of the things that don't get done today. Depending on your business, there could easily be many more opportunities to reduce costs. Now we will share some of the most impactful cost savings we see in our work with clients.

Communicating with partners. If you are still sending physical mailings with printed materials, catalogs, specs and price schedules, you might consider migrating some or all this information online. If you're not ready to do this, you can at least pilot an experiment and see what feedback you receive. You will probably discover that your customers and partners appreciate that they can have access to up-to-date information online, all the time. The ability to be nimble with real-time changes and savings from printing and postage has the potential to provide substantial savings to your business.

Traditional advertising. There is still certainly a place for traditional advertising, but you should be carefully looking at whether the costs involved with yellow page ads, tradeshows and trade magazines still make sense. We recommend to our clients that before cutting these tactics completely, they ratchet their usage down incrementally to see what impact is felt. Run a smaller ad or host a smaller booth and see if this change causes any negative ramifications. In most cases, it won't, and you'll have savings you can invest in more modern, measurable marketing efforts. Another big advantage of digital marketing is that digital "artifacts" can live on indefinitely. Unlike the ad you place in a trade magazine, which has a finite lifespan, content in the digital world can be presented to new prospects and potential employees for as long as you like.

Eliminating duplicate entry. Here's an important insight that you probably know but may not pay much attention to. Your team members *hate* having to enter the same information over and over into different systems, but it happens all the time. Not only is this kind of work painful for your team, it can really mess up your reporting and data integrity. Finding ways to simplify your data entry will make your employees happier and the data you use to make decisions will be more accurate. We call that a win-win.

Collaboration across time zones. If you have people or customers in different time zones, especially internationally, digital can create better and more affordable opportunities for team collaboration. People can interact in real-time or in online collaboration portals, which can be created to allow team members to work on their schedule. When travel and communication hassles are reduced, you will have a team of workers in disparate locations that work better together. You should also see a reduction in labor costs.

Customer service efficiencies. Using an online chat, email and social channels to handle customer service needs can provide a dramatic improvement in efficiency and customer satisfaction. For common requests, your customer service reps can handle multiple inquiries simultaneously using pre-canned responses that have been carefully reviewed in advance. It's not uncommon for a customer care professional to be able to handle 3-5 times, or more, customer inquiries using these digital tools. Many customers prefer this method of communication as well.

Printed Catalogs. Determining whether to continue printing catalogs is a common question for many of our clients. The answer will depend on several factors. Most companies are scaling back on the production of catalogs, primarily because customers today are willing (and actually prefer) to go online to search for products and information. Sure, for some industries it still makes sense to produce catalogs, at least for now. The advantages of moving away from catalogs include the ability to display new products whenever they become available, remove products that are no longer available without having to wait until the next catalog run and, obviously, the printing and postage costs. Online catalogs can be easily customized for specific audiences, making them more relevant and effective at generating incremental sales.

We are confident that there are some things you are doing in your business that could benefit from a digital review. For a long time, we heard that eliminating catalogs was unimaginable for many businesses, but now, a majority of customers appreciate the ability to do a criteria-based search for products and pricing in real-time without having to lug around a big catalog. This is one example of many, but it illustrates the point. Today, conducting business online is often more acceptable and more desired than traditional methods of communicating. Don't be afraid to experiment with some of these ideas. You'll likely find that you can save money in the long run and increase satisfaction on the part of your constituents.

Take some time to talk with your customer service people to see
if they are having to enter data in duplicate systems twice (or
more often) to do their jobs. You'll probably hear several
instances of this kind of duplication. If so, document the specific
scenarios and investigate what can be done to remedy these time
wasters. If your customer service folks can't identify any
duplication, they'll surely have other ideas on how to make their
work more efficient.

Section 3 – GROWING Your E-Commerce

CHALLENGE:
Exploring international opportunities

Selling products into foreign markets used to require a series of time-consuming and often mysterious processes. Today, the Internet makes international sales and marketing much easier and far more transparent. Learn how you can evaluate whether going international makes sense for your organization.

The prospect of growing internationally is an exciting thought for many companies, but there are a number of considerations that must be resolved before any serious move in this direction can be made. For example, if your products require special handling, sales engineering consultation to select the right configuration, or on-site setup and ongoing service, you'll probably need to seek local representation. On the other hand, the barriers to selling online can be dramatically reduced if your team can easily accept orders and ship your products directly to end consumers in international locations. If your organization wants to test whether its products are viable in international markets, trials can begin in relatively short order.

Depending on your business and past experience with handling international orders, we have some recommendations to help you get started:

> *Start in Canada.* We recommend that you start marketing your products in Canada. Depending on your company's circumstances, your internal team may be able to handle the sales and fulfillment activities themselves or you can seek a qualified sales partner there. Selling your equipment into Canada may mandate some modifications to your E-Commerce platform because of currency, provincial and postal code differences. If you're interested

in selling into eastern Canada, you will have to deal with dual languages, as well (English and French). Canada offers a great opportunity to explore international business and give you the chance to see, first hand, how the unique processes involved in doing business outside the USA impact your organization. Assuming your team finds success selling your products into Canada, you can then look at expanding into other markets around the world.

Dropdown list of languages or flags. Another way to approach international sales is to create a dropdown list of languages or flag icons that indicate multiple languages on your primary website. As an initial phase, allow visitors who select a language variant to view a single page of text in their native language that directs them to call your home office customer service or a local, in-country sales representative that can speak with them. You can track how many visits and requests come from this page and decide whether it makes sense to expand the language offering to additional content or provide the full company and product specification information in the applicable languages. If the sales opportunities support the addition of more languages, by all means, make that happen. If not, at least you won't have spent the time and energy to fully translate your content.

For content translation, particularly for complex equipment, engage technical experts who are fluent in the native language. With improving artificial intelligence software this may change, but currently, the use of automated translation tools isn't recommended. Improper grammar and phraseology mistakes are common with these tools, which can make your company look bad to the very audience you're trying to attract.

Conduct a competitive analysis. As you get started with international business or seek to expand into new international markets more broadly, it's a good idea to perform a competitive analysis to see what other companies are selling into the desired geographical area. As a starting point, perform a Google search on the types of products and services you offer and see what results are displayed. You'll need to search in both English, which is the international language of business, and the native language for the country you are reviewing. You should be able to quickly see what organizations are offering similar products and services. If you think there's an opportunity for your business, you'll obviously want to seek good legal advice in the country you're targeting. Specific standards, laws and specialized government requirements often apply to companies that distribute products into international markets. Consumer laws vary drastically from country to country. It's vital that you pay attention to the legal and regulatory conditions, so you don't end up with a big mess on your hands.

Establish a local/regional partner. If you want to avoid selling directly to consumers in foreign lands, another common option is to establish a local or regional partner who can stock and service your products. In this case, you may choose to turn overall sales, marketing, fulfillment and customer service functions. You may opt to build and manage the E-Commerce website on behalf of your local partner to absorb costs and to keep an eye on what they're doing for your business. Otherwise, you can have your internal team maintain some of these functions. Every situation is different and careful testing can help navigate these new waters successfully. Not unlike developing sales leads, some companies seek new dealers by running Google Ads pay-per-click campaigns and other programmatic digital ad campaigns that target prospective in-country partners.

Use global internet partners. Several companies with whom we've worked leverage global internet partners like Amazon and eBay to sell their products into all parts of the world. It may not be an ideal solution long-term, as the fees paid to these resellers can be high, but the process is easy to manage and using this type of service can get your company into international business within days.

Be mindful of GDPR and other, similar privacy requirements. As we discussed in Section 1 of this book, working in places like Europe requires special attention to strict privacy laws. Failure to do this right could mean hefty fines for your business. Canada, for example, has much more strict email marketing regulations. US companies that don't realize these differences—or choose to ignore the mandates—can end up learning expensive lessons. Because these regulations are constantly changing, find a partner that is well-versed in this area and then pay close attention to their guidance.

If your company has never done international business, you'll want to proceed at a slower pace to make sure you understand the complexities. If you experience a few bumps and bruises along the journey, don't give up. The results can be very positive for your company. For quite a number of US organizations, their international sales exceed domestic sales. If you've done things correctly, the Internet will make it easy for customers to find you and for your team to conduct business anywhere in the world in real-time.

Invest in the creation of a new landing page that covers one of the products you make. Focus on a specific international market and find someone to properly translate the information into the local language. Offer product uses that fit the selected country's unique situation. For most markets, you'll want to display product specifications using metric measurements. The more specific you can be with your content, the easier it will be for prospective customers to find you online.

Monitor inbound calls and inquiries to see if it makes sense to expand efforts with additional landing pages, a regional microsite or a full country-specific E-Commerce website.

Section 3 – GROWING Your E-Commerce

CHALLENGE:
Humanizing your brand story
Can your customers and partners tell your business apart from your competitors? If you're looking for ways to differentiate and find customers who are cheerleaders for your brand, you'll want to learn how online efforts can help accomplish this important mission.

Telling your brand story in a compelling manner is a long-term commitment, but with today's modern communication channels it's also easier than ever to do. Let's say that upfront. Never before have you had a medium in which you can share your brand story more effectively, efficiently and powerfully. Let's outline how digital can support the communication of your brand and lead to new customers and more sales.

Understand that your company needs to share information about the products you build or sell to people who currently use your products and to prospects you want to use your products in the future. If you work with sales channel partners, your goal is to find new dealers and cultivate them. Doing this will help reinforce why your products are the best fit for their customers.

In the past, telling your company's brand story meant running expensive ads in the phone book, newspapers and magazines or on the radio, TV and billboards. You might have sent direct mail pieces or catalogs to your mailing list of customers and prospects, but because of the high costs involved, inherently these efforts were generally focused more on strong sales language than brand building.

Today, you can bring your company's personality and culture to life by using one or more of the many online digital channels. Not only can you tell your story, you can reveal it by sharing engaging information over a period of time. Best of all, the expenses associated with this kind of marketing are typically modest.

Using your website, Facebook, LinkedIn and YouTube channels, to name a few, you can share your company's story using creative anecdotes, fun photos, infographics and videos. Not only can you tell your story, you can retell it often, so people think of your company in a positive light. Through pure love of your brand or using engaging contests, you can get customers to share their testimonials and product usage videos.

Because of the flexibility and relatively low cost of using digital marketing, you can introduce new products more quickly and begin building interest, even before new equipment is available for sale on your website or in stores.

Don't be afraid to have your digital team try new ideas to see what works and what doesn't. If you show your business as genuine and not phony, your audience will allow you to make mistakes as you determine how to best use online channels to connect with them.

You can also detail your company's history and culture, something few companies would have been able to afford to do in the past. Funny stories from your organization's past and old photos of founders, employees and facilities are often interesting to your digital constituents.

Another concept we've seen work well is a "meet and greet" website section, where online visitors can interact with someone inside your company. Perhaps you had a "Meet Linda" section in your printed company newsletter, but it was not very dynamic. Allowing your customers, partners and prospects to see the type of people they will work with is a great way to engage relationship between people. It can also be a lot of fun to showcase special interests, historical facts and more.

Let's be clear that sharing this kind of information across social media channels is not free, but with the wide reach of current fans and the possibility of exponential sharing, this method of showing off your company and its people is relatively inexpensive.

A few of the clients we work with are unsure of social media. They often come to us thinking that social efforts are a waste of time. While we sympathize with this attitude, it couldn't be farther from the truth. It may be more difficult to quantify specific sales—though not impossible—but this kind of marketing can endear your company to the people you need to grow sales. When folks see your business as a collection of people doing good things, you'll be in a position to win more business and attract more employees. It may take some time to ramp up social interaction but when done correctly, the benefits can be powerful.

As you go about sharing your story, take time to "listen" as well. Getting feedback from your customers can change everything. The "Letters to the Editor" of the past have been replaced by instant feedback. You can monitor comments about your organization, interact with your visitors and find new ways to connect and serve.

Your company's ability to create and share videos rather than use static pictures and text makes all the difference. Whether it is a product demonstration or a culture-centric video about a recent volunteering day your team did together, the ease of producing decent quality video today should be amazing to anyone who has been in marketing for longer than a few years.

As you think about your brand, remember that it's an ongoing story. In the past, there was no affordable way to produce, deliver or share rich brand information to a large audience. To be effective, you have to make the commitment to continually share your brand story. When executed well, sharing your brand can be among the most successful elements of your marketing strategy, but be realistic about the short-term effect that brand stories will have on your sales. For most organizations, this kind of effort is definitely a marathon, not a sprint. Your team should still be able to gauge some key metrics of effectiveness much more quickly than you could have dreamed of ten years ago.

If your company uses social media and you have not yet produced a video, do so. Don't worry about making it a highly produced affair. Film a how-to video and make a social post indicating that you have had questions from your customers about the topic covered. Be sure and include a link to your online store, where interested visitors can buy equipment and parts.

If this doesn't meet your needs, congratulate a longstanding employee on an anniversary and post it as a sign of stability in your company. A post like this is also a statement to potential employees that you provide a great place to work. Odds are either of these posts will outperform the average text or image-based message, because people like to see social media content that reflects an organization's genuine personality and culture.

Section 3 – GROWING Your E-Commerce

CHALLENGE:
Transitioning to the next generation
Over the next few years, thousands of business owners will be transitioning their companies to new and younger managers. Learn how online reporting can play a big role in making this process more efficient and successful.

There's no doubt that a lot of business owners and leaders are working towards—or worrying about—a major transition to future leaders in the coming years. If you're wondering how the Internet and E-Commerce can help with this important issue, we're happy to share our experience. We know that this topic can involve difficult discussions, but these tactics can help make the process go much more smoothly.

Younger people expect to do more work functions online. Because today's up-and-coming business leaders have grown up with the Internet, they're far more comfortable with it than most of their predecessors. New business managers expect to use the web for almost everything they do. They want to have access from anywhere and at any time to the information they need to make prudent business decisions. In the last decade we've seen younger business leaders, often family members, go from learners to valuable contributors. These managers are pushing for the changes that are needed to convert old-fashioned business into modern, web-driven organizations. Just like the change in manufacturing processes over the past 25 years, business operations are either migrating to modern practices or they're likely on track to die a slow death.

Looking back, we have encountered a lot of younger workers who have been frustrated by their employers (company owners), who weren't ready or willing to invest in online activities. Fortunately, this attitude has been steadily changing for the better and these companies are in better shape from a sales and marketing perspective for it.

Your business will be worth more if you're using digital tactics in the right way. If you're thinking of selling your business, there's almost always a higher valuation attributed to those companies that embrace digital technology. The reasons are simple. Companies that can connect online with their constituents have a greater flow of information, an increased opportunity to sell more products and the ability to build market share more rapidly. They will also be able to hire more qualified employees. If you don't believe us, talk to a business broker who has recent experience selling businesses. A modest investment in digital can mean a significant return on investment.

You can solve one of your biggest challenges by embracing online technologies. Think about the future, when you won't be leading your company. We imagine that one of your greatest concerns may be the sharing of your deep business experience with the new leadership team. Leveraging the Internet, you can get all the customer data, business know-how and processes into places where that knowledge can be accessed, consumed and enhanced by new leaders. Workflows can be created to make certain that business processes are followed and documented. Digital assets can be cataloged to ensure that your historical documents, records and plans are available when and where needed. While some of this history may not be deemed valuable by the next generation, there will surely come a time when at least some of it is needed to ensure a smooth transition.

You can keep connected to your business during the transition in ways you never could in the past. We understand that it's hard to walk away from the business you've built, grown and cared for, but having a connection to the new leadership using modern online tools can make the transition easier to handle. These tools eliminate the time and expense of travel and make impromptu meetings easy to conduct. In addition to the meetings themselves, you can have access to online E-Commerce reporting that keeps you in the loop on the business metrics you deem important. Having a dashboard of key performance indicators that are pulled from the various software tools used in your business will enable you to monitor your company in near real-time and hold your successors accountable for the decisions they're making.

Transitioning your business to the next generation will certainly require a lot of time and effort. While bringing your business into the modern, digital age won't help solve all of the challenges you face, it is an important step in making sure your company is well prepared for the next generation.

Talk to an upcoming business leader whom you are grooming to take over a key role in your organization and ask for their ideas for modernizing the business. Find out how they currently view the sales and marketing of your products. See if they have a desire to elevate your business' online activities in ways you may have not yet considered.

Business today has brought a vast amount of technology to throughput, inventory and fulfillment processes, but still too few are leveraging the communication and marketing capabilities that the Internet provides. If you allow your upcoming leadership to be candid with you, we expect you'll learn what they view as important when thinking about taking over the management of day-to-day operations.

About the Authors

We've been business partners since 1996. We started with a few technical developers and created Spindustry, a web development and digital marketing agency. Back then, most of our competitors were graphic designers, so we carved a niche for handling complex data needs using proficient programmers. We helped insurance companies take their rate tables and move them from quarterly mailings to an online agent portal that provided real-time rates and commission information. The company no longer had to wait to adjust rates based on market conditions and the competition—they could make changes instantly. Since those early days, we've grown the business to include enterprise E-Commerce development capabilities, handling transactions totaling millions of dollars each day. Our team also designs, builds and manages large websites and customer portals that offer deep user engagement and functionalities. Our digital marketing team connects our clients' E-Commerce sites with interested buyers.

Interestingly, Michael and I had similar upbringings, moving several times as our fathers were transferred to new job locations. The experience of moving multiple times certainly helped us adapt well to the many business opportunities and situations that we've encountered along our journey.

I have been married for nearly 35 years to my wife, Jan, and have two grown daughters, Erin and Kyra. I graduated from Iowa State University with a degree in Graphic Design and an emphasis in Journalism and Mass Communications. Fortunately, I've had the opportunity to see much of the world, traveling both for business and pleasure.

Michael has been married for nearly 25 years to his wife, Lora, and has two school-aged kids, Aidan and Alyssa. Michael graduated from the University of Colorado with degrees in Management Information Systems and Marketing. He is a serious Star Wars fan with an enviable collection of several thousand related toys.

In 2016 we wrote a bestselling book about digital

marketing for manufacturers and distributors, called *RUN GROW TRANSFORM | A Manufacturer's Guide to Digital Marketing*. While that book was and still is appropriate as a general marketing guide, this book focuses much more on E-Commerce and how it can provide companies of all sizes with new online sales opportunities.

We truly love to help companies of all types, especially manufacturers, distributors and retailers find ways to improve sales, position their brand, recruit great new employees and so much more by implementing well-designed and well-executed E-Commerce and digital marketing strategies.

Prior to starting Spindustry, we worked together for several years at an export management company. We served US manufacturers in building and supporting international sales and marketing activities. It's amazing how much has changed in the years since we left that business. Back then the fax machine was revolutionary. Sending literature to a distributor in Asia involved expensive courier services that often took days and phone calls were terribly expensive. Connecting manufacturers with international distributors and end consumers required a great deal of knowledge and effort. With modern business technologies, the divide between product builders and product users has become very narrow.

In the years we have worked together, we've found some pretty good success. Our companies have been named to the *Inc. 500* and *Inc. 5000* Lists of the fastest-growing, privately-held companies in America. Based in Des Moines, we were very excited when the *Des Moines Register* named our firm, Spindustry Digital, the #1 Top Place to Work in the state of Iowa in 2013.

We are blessed with many more awards and honors, but the greatest joy we receive in our work is the success our clients achieve with the help of our team's efforts. Working with our client partners makes our efforts in the digital world worthwhile and rewarding.

To the continuing advancement of your business in the digital world, we wish you and your company all the best.

Steve and Michael